THE LEARNING SCIENCES IN THE SECONDARY CLASSROOM

THE LEARNING SCIENCES IN THE SECONDARY CLASSROOM

JAMES SHEA
AUDREY WOOD
STEPHEN COX

A PRACTICAL GUIDE FOR TRAINEE TEACHERS

3rd Floor
HYLO
103–105 Bunhill Row
London, EC1Y 8LZ
UK

2455 Teller Road
Thousand Oaks
California 91320

10th Floor, Emaar Capital Tower
2 MG Road, Sikanderpur, Sector 26
Gurugram, Haryana – 122002
India

8 Marina View Suite 43-053
Asia Square Tower 1
Singapore 018960

Editor: Amy Thornton
Senior project editor: Chris Marke
Cover design: Wendy Scott
Typeset by: C&M Digitals (P) Ltd, Chennai, India
Printed in the UK

Library of Congress Control Number: 2026934484

British Library Cataloguing in Publication Data

A catalogue record for this book is available from the
British Library

ISBN 978-1-5296-8749-1
ISBN 978-1-5296-8748-4 (pbk)

CONTENTS

ABOUT THE AUTHORS

Dr James Shea is a Principal Lecturer and the Initial Teacher Education Portfolio Leader at the University of Bedfordshire, overseeing all undergraduate and postgraduate teacher education programmes. His primary focus is on educating teachers and collaborating with partnership schools through research and teacher education. He is a highly awarded academic whose research expertise covers key areas in cognitive science, including retrieval practice and the use of cognitive load theory in teaching, as well as GCSE student revision strategies. He is a Trustee for the Pyramid Multi Academy Trust and serves as an External Examiner for the University of Cambridge. He also chairs several key university committees. You can follow him on X™ (formerly Twitter) @englishspecial.

Stephen Cox is a Lecturer in Education (Science) and the PGCE Secondary Science Lead Mentor at the University of Bedfordshire. He is a highly experienced educator, having spent 15 years as a science and drama teacher, covering biology, chemistry, physics and applied science across all secondary key stages. His dual background – with a science specialism in biology (ecology) and a drama focus on physical theatre – provides him with a unique and valuable pedagogical perspective. Having held various roles, including head of year, head of department and in-school mentor, his current work involves leading the secondary science teacher education course. He supports trainee teachers and shares his deep knowledge and passion for evidence-informed practice, focusing on developing practical, subject-specific pedagogical knowledge in future teachers.

Dr Audrey Wood is a Senior Lecturer in Teacher Education and the course leader for postgraduate secondary teacher education at the University of Bedfordshire. Her expertise is built on 15 years of teaching secondary English in comprehensive schools, before moving into initial teacher education (ITE) at the University of Huddersfield, where she led the Secondary English PGCE and managed various employment-based ITE courses.

Prior to her teaching career, Dr Wood had a successful career in adult mental health and general nursing, specialising in accident and emergency care. This unique background inspired her PhD research, which focused on the experiences of career changers – specifically military personnel – transitioning into secondary school teaching. She continues to supervise dissertations and is a valuable contributor to primary and secondary ITE programmes. Follow her on X (formerly Twitter) @AudersbyGoode.

PART 1

1
INTRODUCTION
USING THE LEARNING SCIENCES IN YOUR TEACHING

LEARNING OUTCOMES

By reading this chapter you will develop:

- An understanding of how this book can be used to help inform your teaching
- The reasons behind why such a book on learning sciences is needed
- How research into learning sciences has remained popular for teachers

INITIAL TEACHER TRAINING AND
EARLY CAREER FRAMEWORK (ITTECF)

The key reading from the ITTECF that is to be explored within this chapter is:

Baddeley, A. (2003). Working memory: looking back and looking forward. *Nature Reviews Neuroscience*, 4(10), 829–39. https://doi.org/10.1038/nrn1201

INTRODUCTION

This book is for trainee and beginning secondary teachers – for those who look at the many textbooks and handbooks on learning sciences and who want a book that cuts through all the different ideas about how teachers should use them in their teaching. It is not an encyclopaedia of all the many and varied learning sciences – there are many books that do that already. Instead, this book seeks to ensure that the polarised debate around learning sciences does not prevent you from teaching to a high standard by using learning sciences in your lessons.

The landscape of education is constantly evolving, but there is no escaping a growing emphasis on evidence-informed practice. While secondary schools in the UK have commendably moved away from poorly evidenced ideas such as learning styles and brain gym, a new and equally complex challenge has emerged: the accurate and effective application of learning sciences in the classroom. Ideas transferred from domains like *cognitive psychology* and *neuroscience* to education have, at times, mutated into inefficient or incorrect practices. The term 'lethal mutations' is often used for these sorts of ideas, but even this term is controversial. The term is borrowed from biology where knowledge is drawn from specific scientific rules. Education is not an exact science regardless of how much empirical data academic studies produce, as each child or school class is different and any scientific 'law' we seek to produce for education will be immediately undermined by the sheer diversity of students that are in schools. Many teachers prefer to keep to more neutral terms such as 'misapplication' or 'implementation drift'. As such, you can see how this book aims to provide a practical and critical guide for teachers to confidently navigate the terrain and terminology of using learning sciences in their teaching.

The Department for Education's (DfE's) 'golden thread' – encompassing the Initial Teacher Training and Early Career Framework (ITTECF) and National Programme of Qualifications (NPQs) – sets out the need for strong evidence to underpin teacher education and development, even though it itself is often criticised for being narrowly ideological in content and research (Shea, 2024). However, despite this foundation of evidence and embedded programmes of study, and regardless of criticism, some schools and teachers continue to grapple with understanding and implementing evidence-informed approaches effectively. For instance, some teachers initiate lessons with retrieval practice primarily for behavioural outcomes, rather than to exploit the test-potentiated effect (Bates and Shea, 2024). Sometimes they even re-teach the material, which defeats the purpose of the strategy and means the new strategy requires more time and resources than that which it replaced. If the school or multi-academy trust (MAT) has imposed these strategies as part of a top-down policy, then this means that misunderstandings about how to implement ideas about learning theories and research can be amplified across the school or trust with resulting lower outcomes both in terms of academic and affective areas, as well as inefficiency being built into every lesson across a trust. Just five minutes wasted from every lesson is a huge resource spend at trust level.

Teachers who implement top-down policies need to understand the academic base from which those policies were developed and must be able to provide robust and critical challenge to such policies if they are indeed being misapplied or implemented in a way which prevents the policy from being a success. In our experience, and across evidence, the lack of autonomy for teachers to adapt implementation can undermine the success of it. Even though you will find a strong emphasis on fidelity, the fact remains that the diversity of students that a teacher meets means that teachers need a degree of autonomy to implement a policy in a way that delivers success for all students rather than limiting some students.

Summarising the landscape, this book was born from the recognition that teachers need not only to understand the theoretical underpinnings of learning sciences, but also to develop the skills necessary to adapt and implement these ideas effectively in their classrooms. Far too many teachers, schools or trusts are relying on pre-packaged curricula without the knowledge or understanding of the evidence which influences the curricula to truly engage with the learning science principles embedded within them, or to tailor them to individual classes and pupils. This handbook is designed to address that need, serving as a working companion for teacher training or for teachers encountering learning science concepts through continued professional development (CPD) or existing curriculum documents, ensuring their teaching is genuinely evidence-informed and critically reviewed.

Rather than attempting to be an exhaustive reference for every learning science theory in existence, this book will focus on the main learning sciences prevalent in secondary schools:

- behaviourism,

- cognitivism (including cognitive science),

- constructivism and

- connectivism.

We will use examples to illustrate how these diverse learning sciences can be blended to develop individual lessons, sequences of lessons and even whole-school planning. The content will address the key readings within the golden thread, supplementing them with additional critical readings to deepen understanding of each learning science and its practical implementation in teaching. For instance, when exploring cognitive load and working memory, we will go beyond Cowan's (2001) well-known 'slots' idea for the limitations of working memory (the idea that your student can only hold four to seven items of information in their working memory at any one time) by also incorporating the alternative 'resolutions' idea proposed by Frick (1988) and Zhang and Luck (2008). If you have only ever met Cowan's 'four to seven' slots idea then the idea of resolution will resonate with you as a teacher, and it is this sort of criticality you will enjoy through accessing this book.

Ultimately, this book will empower you to learn the knowledge and develop the skills necessary to accurately implement and investigate learning sciences within your teaching, fostering a more effective and impactful classroom environment and preparing you for advanced qualifications like the Chartered College of Teaching's Chartered Teacher qualification. It is a guide to transforming secondary teaching by truly harnessing the power of learning sciences.

ADAPTING TO TOP-DOWN POLICIES

A good starting point for you is to think about a top-down policy in your school or MAT and reflect on why it is there. Rather than consider the theory first, consider the policy first.

For example, many schools have explicit routines governing how children will move and *behave* around the school at specific times of the day or during specific events. These routines are integral to how the school is run and any deviance from these routines is strictly prohibited – either by staff or pupils. Sanctions to be applied for those who do not follow the routines are set by the school or trust in a behaviour management policy. Such routines can be as simple as how students line up and enter a classroom or complex, detailing how staff and students will move during a fire alarm. Indeed, schools will practise drills rather than rely on everyone knowing what to do through simply reading a policy – and this is classic *operant conditioning* from the behaviourism side of learning sciences.

Think about the entering of a classroom. Imagine the school you work for has asked you to be at the door when your pupils enter the classroom; that they line up outside the classroom and remove any coats before entering in silence; that you perform a uniform check on their entry; and that they sit down at their desk, get their equipment out and immediately undertake a task such as a 'do now' or 'bell work'. Why has the school set this strict behaviour policy? Why can't teachers just have their own policies?

Being at the door means you have control over not just your teaching space, but the way pupils behave outside your classroom. It ensures pupils are consistently managed in their entry to the classroom. If each teacher had their own policy, the students would likely have a dozen different routines to remember and would end up deviant outside one classroom and compliant outside another with identical behaviour. One teacher might not mind coats on, while another is issuing sanctions for them wearing their coats. Behaviourist operant conditioning works best when the discriminative stimuli (the cues that signal whether a behaviour will be reinforced or sanctioned) and the resulting consequences are applied consistently across contexts. This allows students to make clear associations between their behaviour and its outcomes, strengthening the desired behaviours through reinforcement or reducing unwanted behaviours through consistent application of sanctions. When all staff align their expectations and responses, students receive a single, unambiguous behavioural framework, reducing cognitive load and making positive behaviours more automatic.

Yet, what if a student does not do the do now task? Do you always immediately sanction every time? If the student *can* do the do now task, then 'yes' would be the answer. However, they might have been absent, they might not have the necessary equipment, or they might require some kind of adaptation by the teacher to enable them to undertake the task. In these cases, the sanction is not appropriate. You can see how a teacher can implement a behaviourist policy with too much fidelity. The school expects the teacher to apply adaptation to the strict behaviourist operant conditioning. Yet, that autonomy is often not written into policies – rather it is seen as central teacher knowledge of the sort learned through qualified teacher status (QTS) training and the early career teacher (ECT) years.

PRACTICAL APPLICATION

A large multi-academy trust serving several secondary schools has implemented a policy requiring every subject to produce and use knowledge organisers for each unit of study. These are single-page, clearly structured summaries containing the key facts, vocabulary, diagrams and timelines students need to master.

CONSIDER THIS: BLENDING IDEAS AND EVIDENCE

Consider the idea that most approaches to teaching and learning blend ideas and evidence from multiple learning sciences rather than being dependent on a single idea from a learning science or a single learning science.

In reflecting on this, think about:

- how can ideas such as cognitive load be combined with the idea of constructing knowledge?
- if a teacher takes the whole class through a specific sequence of learning activities, using precise resources, where do the ideas of both cognitivism and constructivism begin to blend?
- can you think of an example of a school policy that was presented as from a learning science, but upon reflection is actually a blend of more than one?

COGNITIVIST FOUNDATIONS

The policy is grounded in cognitivism, particularly the principles of schema development and the reduction of cognitive load. By presenting essential information in a concise, consistent format, the knowledge organisers act as an external memory aid, helping students encode knowledge into long-term memory and retrieve it efficiently. The use of repeated, low-stakes retrieval activities directly aligns with the cognitivist focus on strengthening memory traces and facilitating transfer to new contexts.

LIMITATIONS AND CHALLENGES

However, deciding who selects the *key knowledge* is not a neutral act. Curriculum leads, subject heads, or classroom teachers inevitably bring their own perspectives, values and interpretations of what is essential – potentially narrowing the curriculum to what is most easily listed rather than what is most conceptually rich. Knowledge organisers can also struggle to account for the varied prior knowledge students bring, meaning that the same knowledge organiser may under-challenge some learners while overwhelming others.

Different types of knowledge also present challenges. Declarative facts and clearly defined processes fit neatly into knowledge organiser boxes, but procedural, conditional and tacit knowledge are harder to capture. In subjects like history or science, the format often works well, as there is a stable body of content to master. In contrast, in English literature, much of the 'novel' knowledge is constructed individually and socially through inference, interpretation and discussion. Here, the knowledge organiser may support some aspects – like recalling quotations or literary terminology – but risks oversimplifying the dynamic, interpretive nature of English literature. Indeed, retrieval practice of *key quotations*, as set out in the knowledge organiser, can lead to an effect known as *retrieval-induced forgetting* (RIF). That is, the memory of the rehearsed key quotations pushes out the memories of all other content preventing students from attaining higher marks in examinations by drawing on a full range of content. Further, *cued recall* of the sort enhanced by retrieval practice can hinder *near and far transfer of knowledge*. In an examination, students will be expected to undertake near and far transfer of knowledge far more often than they will need to undertake specific cued recall. Those questions are generally the easier questions at the start of a tapered section of an examination. An overfocus on specific cued recall rather than near and far transfer could lead to poor recall of wider knowledge and reduced near and far transfer – the very opposite of what the trust is trying to do.

FIDELITY OF IMPLEMENTATION

For the policy to be effective without becoming reductive, certain elements must be delivered with precision. Knowledge organisers need to be accurate, curriculum-aligned and carefully sequenced to build on prior knowledge. They must be supplemented with opportunities for discussion, inference-making and problem-solving, especially in subjects where meaning is co-constructed. Retrieval activities should connect the knowledge organiser's content to higher-order tasks, rather than treating the knowledge organiser as the sole repository of learning. What is especially important is that students are offered opportunities to practice near and far recall of information through a range of teaching and learning activities to prevent issues of near and far transfer.

BALANCING COGNITIVISM AND CONSTRUCTIVISM

The trust actively works to integrate constructivist principles alongside the cognitivist structure of the policy. For example, English departments use knowledge organisers to reinforce key terminology and quotations, but lessons explore the knowledge and beyond through discussion and collaborative analysis, where students co-construct interpretations that go beyond the knowledge organiser's content. Furthermore, they practice *free recall* frequently to reduce RIF and ensure the same information is required for multiple contexts to enhance near and far transfer. In science, knowledge organisers serve as a base for practical investigations where students test, refine and sometimes challenge the factual knowledge they've memorised.

By acknowledging the limitations of the format and deliberately building in spaces for knowledge construction, the policy aims to harness the strengths of both cognitivism and constructivism – providing students with secure, retrievable knowledge while still encouraging them to think critically, make connections and create new understanding of the sort that enables near and far transfer as well as preventing retrieval-based forgetting.

CHAPTER SUMMARY

School and trust-wide policies often draw upon principles from the learning sciences, aiming to create consistent, predictable conditions for learning. Behaviourist-informed routines, such as standardised entry procedures, demonstrate how consistency in cues and consequences strengthens desired behaviours. Yet these same routines require professional judgement to avoid over-application; teachers need autonomy to adapt expectations when circumstances make strict fidelity counterproductive.

Similarly, policies grounded in cognitivism, such as the trust-wide use of knowledge organisers, offer powerful tools for building schemas, reducing cognitive load and improving retrieval. However, they carry inherent limitations: decisions about what counts as key knowledge are value-laden; certain subjects, such as English literature, rely heavily on knowledge constructed through inference and discussion; and overemphasis on rehearsed recall can hinder near and far transfer or cause RIF.

The most effective school-wide policies therefore blend fidelity to core principles with space for teacher autonomy based on knowledge of the limitations of learning sciences. This balance allows schools to preserve the benefits of consistency while accommodating the realities of subject-specific pedagogy, varied prior knowledge and the need for students to engage in both the secure retrieval of facts and the construction of new understanding.

REFLECTIVE QUESTIONS: CHAPTER 1

Can you think of a school or trust-wide rule or policy that was founded upon an idea or ideas from learning sciences?

- How do you know that a learning science was drawn upon for the policy?
- What elements of the policy must be implemented with fidelity?
- What examples of the autonomy needed for the policy to be a success can you think of?

⸺ FURTHER READING ⸺

ITTECF 2.6 Pupils have different working memory capacities; some pupils with SEND may have more limited working memory capacity than their peers without SEND.

Carroll, J., Bradley, L., Crawford, H., Hannant, P., Johnson, H. and Thompson, A. (2017).

SEN Support: A Rapid Evidence Assessment. Available at:

Carroll_SENSupportARapidEvidenceAssessment.pdf

Carroll et al. present a rapid evidence assessment of effective practices for supporting children and young people on special educational needs (SEN) support in schools and post-16 institutions. The report synthesises existing research to identify strategies that enhance outcomes for these SEN students. It highlights that effective SEN support relies on collaboration among teachers, support staff and families, ensuring a holistic approach to each student's development. Tailoring interventions to meet individual needs, rather than adopting a one-size-fits-all model, is emphasised as crucial for achieving better outcomes. The authors also note that ongoing professional development for teachers enhances their capacity to support diverse learners, and that regular monitoring and evaluation of interventions allows support to remain relevant and effective. Overall, the report underscores the importance of evidence-based, personalised approaches that promote inclusive educational environments.

▬ REFERENCES ▬

Bates, G. and **Shea, J.** (2024). Retrieval practice in the wild. *Mind, Brain and Education, 18*(3), 249–57.

Cowan, N. (2001). The magical number 4 in short-term memory: a reconsideration of mental storage capacity. *Behavioral and Brain Sciences, 24*(1), 87–185.

Frick, R. W. (1988). The capacity of visual working memory: a slot model. *Journal of Experimental Psychology: Human Perception and Performance, 14*(1), 1–22. https://doi.org/10.1037/0096-1523.14.1.1

Shea, J. (2024). How reforms of teacher education challenge principles of social justice. In **J. Wearmouth**, **U. Maylor**, **K. Lindley** and **J. Shea** (eds), *Social Justice in Education*. New York: McGraw Hill, pp. 39–55.

Zhang, W. and **Luck, S. J.** (2008). Discrete fixed-resolution representations in visual working memory. *Nature, 453*(7192), 233–5. https://doi.org/10.1038/nature06860

2

THE RISE OF LEARNING SCIENCES IN TEACHING

LEARNING OUTCOMES

By reading this chapter you will develop:

- An understanding of the evolution of learning sciences over the past 50 years and the contributions of key theorists such as Vygotsky, Piaget, Skinner, Kirschner, Sweller, Baddeley, Cowan, Siemens and Downes
- Insight into how different learning theories - constructivism, behaviourism, cognitivism and connectivism - have influenced teaching practices and educational strategies
- Confidence in applying these learning theories to design effective and inclusive lesson plans that leverage modern technology and cater to diverse student needs

INITIAL TEACHER TRAINING AND EARLY CAREER FRAMEWORK (ITTECF)

The key reading from the ITTECF that is to be explored within this chapter is:

Baddeley, A. (2003). Working memory: looking back and looking forward. *Nature Reviews Neuroscience, 4*(10), 829-39. https://doi.org/10.1038/nrn1201

Sweller, J., van Merriënboer, J. J. G. and Paas, F. G. W. C. (1998). Cognitive architecture and instructional design. *Educational Psychology Review, 10*(3), 251-96. https://doi.org/10.1023/A:1022193728205

INTRODUCTION

Learning sciences profoundly influence how teachers and schools design curricula and the pedagogical approaches they use. Over the past 50 years, the field has evolved significantly from the traditional foundation of behaviourism and constructivism and now incorporates ideas from cognitivism as well as connectivism. This book, and indeed this chapter, is not a reference book for all theories of learning. Instead, it tries to capture how theories of learning influence teaching and how they have become so influential or popular. This chapter will also cover the contributions of key theorists such as Vygotsky, Piaget, Bruner and Skinner, alongside the emergence of cognitivism and connectivism, to illustrate how these diverse theories have shaped teaching practices and educational strategies over the past 50 years.

SOCIAL CONSTRUCTIVISM

New teachers in training are still introduced to foundational theories such as Vygotsky's (1978) social constructivist learning, which emphasises the importance of social interaction and the zone of proximal development (ZPD) where the teacher enables pupils to access learning that is not accessible when a teacher (or more capable peer) is not present. However, they can meet quite a different message in the secondary schools where they teach. Some schools have railed hard against social constructivism in the name of group work. It is not unusual to find departments or indeed whole schools or trusts that have a 'no group work' policy. Nevertheless, oral interaction between a teacher and their class remains the dominant model of teaching and teachers operate in the ZPD with their class even if the idea of independent group work has been much reduced. What happens less, therefore, is the group work concept of Vygotsky's original premise:

> what we call the zone of proximal development. It is the distance between the actual developmental level as determined by independent problem solving and the level of potential development as determined through problem solving ... in collaboration with more capable peers.

> (Vygotsky, 1978, p. 87)

In many schools, only the teacher acts as the more capable peer rather than fellow students. This is because of the stigma attached to group work by cognitivists who blame poor group work for increased extraneous load. While this is a valid criticism, eschewing group work simply because one thinks they cannot deliver it effectively is akin to eschewing questioning because one cannot conduct question and answer sessions to a high standard. A better position to take is to insist that where group work takes place, it must be of a high standard and involve work which can only be undertaken collaboratively rather than by a single person.

Teachers in training still learn about Piaget's (1952) stages of cognitive development, which emphasise the importance of aligning learning activities with pupils' developmental levels. Piaget described how children construct new knowledge by assimilating new information into existing schemata or accommodating their schemata to incorporate new experiences. While influential, Piaget's stage theory has been critiqued for its emphasis on discrete stages, and contemporary research suggests a more continuous developmental process. Nevertheless, his work highlights the impact of age and biological maturation on cognitive development and learning. The assimilation of powerful knowledge as children grow older is a key feature of the curriculum in England today and is directly influenced by the work on the sociological concept of *powerful knowledge* from Young (2010, 2011) whose ideas affected the reform of the national curriculum for England (Gove, 2012). This idea of learning specific powerful knowledge and constructing it into schemata led to the emphasis in the English school system on the assimilation of knowledge as part of a Department for Education (DfE) (Gibb, 2017a, b) push to bring the ideas of Hirsch (1987, 1996, 2006) into the curriculum.

Prospective teachers will also explore curriculum planning through the lens of Bruner's (1960) *spiral curriculum*. This model, much like Piaget's (1952) work on cognitive development, emphasises the active role of the learner in constructing knowledge. Bruner posited that learning is not a linear accumulation of facts, but rather a process of building upon and refining existing understanding. The spiral curriculum advocates for revisiting key concepts repeatedly throughout a student's education, each time at a deeper level of complexity and abstraction. As students progress through their school years, they encounter familiar ideas in new contexts, allowing them to make connections, expand their schema and develop a more nuanced grasp of the subject matter. This approach aligns with constructivist principles, recognising that learners actively interpret and organise information rather than passively absorbing it. By revisiting concepts in a spiral fashion, teachers can cater to the evolving cognitive abilities of their students, scaffolding learning and promoting deeper understanding. However, like Piaget's stage theory, Bruner's model has also been subject to critique. Some argue that it can be challenging to implement effectively in practice, as it requires careful planning and coordination, especially if a teacher must adapt for a diverse range of learners who have different starting points and sharply contrasting schemata. Others point out that it may not be suitable for all subjects or learning objectives. Despite these criticisms, the spiral curriculum remains a valuable framework for thinking about how to structure learning experiences in a way that promotes long-term retention and deeper conceptual understanding (Marsh, 2017).

BEHAVIOURISM

Another foundational part of all new teachers' learning is to ensure they understand Skinner's (1953) behaviourist principles, particularly *operant conditioning*, which focuses on how consequences, both reinforcing and punishing, shape behaviour. While often simplified as a system of rewards and sanctions, Skinner's work highlights the importance of carefully considering the *contingencies* between actions and their outcomes. Every school in England has a behaviour management policy, and these policies, while varying in their approach, implicitly or explicitly rely upon principles of operant conditioning, often utilising both positive reinforcement (rewards) and negative reinforcement (removal of an unpleasant stimulus) to encourage desired behaviours, and punishment (application of an aversive stimulus) and response cost (removal of a positive stimulus) to discourage undesirable ones. You will often see a controversial 'moral panic' story in local news of a school that has prevented a child from attending a leavers' prom due to poor behaviour prior to the event. It is important for teachers to understand the potential impact and ethical considerations associated with the use of these techniques. Furthermore, research in behavioural economics has demonstrated the powerful influence of loss aversion, the principle that the pain of a *loss* is psychologically more potent than the pleasure of an equivalent gain. This has significant implications for behaviour management, as studies suggest that the motivational impact of avoiding a loss can be substantially greater than that of achieving a reward (Tversky and Kahneman, 1992). In short, a student will comply with an instruction more readily to avoid losing pre-existing merits than they will to achieve merits.

COGNITIVISM

In addition to these traditional theories, contemporary teacher education now includes cognitivist perspectives. It is important to note that the ITTECF does not have the latest papers from cognitivism, and this can create some theoretical conflicts. Sweller et al.'s (2019) *cognitive load theory* (CLT) provides insights into how instructional design can optimise learning by managing cognitive load, but the 1998 paper which is in the ITTECF contains the earlier work on germane load which Sweller and others have moved away from. In addition, Baddeley's (2000) model of working memory, again which features in the ITTECF, underscores the importance of understanding memory processes in learning whereas Willingham (2017), whose work features strongly in the ITTECF, says that teachers do not need to learn about working memory and that a simple folk psychology model is sufficient. The Baddeley and Willingham sources are therefore in theoretical conflict with each other. As such, the literature base for the ITTECF should not be seen as a defining body of work that teachers use at the exclusion of other wider reading and research – especially for understanding cognitivism.

COGNITIVE LOAD THEORY

Currently, CLT continues to shape educational practice in England. It informs curriculum development, influencing the sequencing and pacing of content. It guides teaching methodologies, encouraging the use of strategies that seek to minimise cognitive overload and promote effective knowledge acquisition. CLT also has implications for assessment, with a growing emphasis on designing assessments that accurately measure learning without imposing unnecessary cognitive demands with an overall focus on creating learning environments that are cognitively *optimised*, allowing students to focus on deep understanding and knowledge construction (Clark and Mayer, 2016). That last word of optimisation is the important part of understanding how CLT is used in schools. The idea is that teachers seek to maximise learning that takes place in their lessons through incorporating their knowledge about CLT into the design of their teaching and learning. However, there is limited research into the effectiveness of the practices that have emerged, and there are considerable fears that ideas known as *mutant practice* have proliferated across the school system, driven by the need to evidence CLT in teaching and learning. Examples of mutant practice include:

- overly simplifying content and reducing desirable difficulty in an attempt to reduce load rather than optimise it;

- misapplying principles of dual coding and the modality effect, such as adding images or auditory information that is poorly coordinated, redundant, or otherwise increases cognitive load rather than reducing it.

LEARNING SCIENCES AND SCHOOL TYPES

There are varied approaches to learning sciences across schools and multi-academy trusts (MATs) in England. Some trusts enforce strict, behaviourist policies in which teaching staff have autonomy to use learning sciences such as social constructivism removed, while others, particularly local authority-maintained schools, allow for greater autonomy and the integration of diverse learning theories. The reason for this division between local authority-maintained schools and schools which are free schools or academies is because practice within MATs has emerged to set an approach to learning theories across all schools in the MAT rather than the local authority-maintained schools' approach which to devolve this decision to the school headteacher.

A recurring theme in this book is the isolation in which these learning sciences are often taught and applied. It should be noted that the rise of cognitivism has been healthy for debate around how learning happens and how teachers should be trained. For a long time, constructivism and behaviourism themselves held sway with teacher educators and, with a limited amount of debate, some ideas were able to penetrate institutions such as the Office for Standards in Education (Ofsted), whose inspectors would habitually comment on seeing what they termed as 'too much teacher talk' and not enough social constructivist discussion. Today, Ofsted inspectors can be found commenting on too much group discussion and not enough explicit instruction, so we can see how ideas from learning sciences have cycled through even such institutions as Ofsted. There is no escaping the fact that learning sciences have permeated far and wide through much of the infrastructure of teaching and learning and the development or inspection of the content within that infrastructure.

PRE-LESSON AND IN-LESSON ADAPTATION

Another theme in this book is that blending learning sciences requires recognising that learning theories cannot universally apply to all students. Teachers must consider these differences when planning lessons or editing pre-existing planning, while making necessary adaptations to ensure inclusivity. In-lesson adaptation is equally important. Teachers must be responsive to students' reactions to teaching which is founded on learning sciences. If your students do not pay sufficient attention, what adaptation should you make? Should you double down on the behaviourist-inspired SLANT (sit up; lean forward; ask and answer questions; nod your head; track the speaker) and issue sanctions for non-compliance? Or should you consider introducing the learning using different ideas if the pre-existing schemata in the class is lower than expected?

It is one of the ongoing issues with reducing teachers' autonomy to decide how to teach. Teachers need the autonomy to adjust the curriculum and teaching strategies to match the diverse needs of their students, ensuring a positive and inclusive learning experience. They also need to consider the era within which they are teaching – with the advent of Artificial Intelligence (AI), large online communities of practice and a proliferation of educational technology, learning sciences still have a contemporary part to play.

CONNECTIVISM AND THE EVOLUTION OF LEARNING NETWORKS

Connectivism, a learning theory proposed by Siemens (2005) and Downes (2008), builds upon earlier socio-constructivist ideas by emphasising the role of digital technology in knowledge acquisition. It suggests that learning is not solely an individual cognitive process, but also occurs across networks of people, technology and information sources. This perspective owes much to the foundational work of Lave and Wenger (1991), who introduced the concept of *communities of practice* (CoP), highlighting the importance of social interaction and situated learning in professional and educational contexts.

Lave and Wenger's (1991) model of CoP proposed that learning is embedded in social environments where individuals participate in shared practices, gaining knowledge through legitimate peripheral participation. This notion was later extended by Wenger (1998) to emphasise the importance of identity formation and community engagement in learning. With the rise of the internet in the late 20th century, these ideas found new applications in online learning communities, where participants could exchange knowledge beyond traditional classroom boundaries. The early 2000s saw the emergence of virtual professional learning networks, discussion forums and social media groups where teachers and students engaged in collaborative knowledge-building. For example, pre-service teachers will connect, via private social media interactions, across boundaries that separate their school placements and teacher education provider to ensure that their learning is enhanced and their ability to pass the Teachers' Standards (DfE, 2013) are secured (Shea, 2019).

Siemens (2005) argued that existing learning theories – such as behaviourism, cognitivism and constructivism – did not sufficiently account for the role of technology in shaping learning experiences. Connectivism emerged as a response, proposing that knowledge is distributed across a network and that the ability to locate and synthesise information is as important as acquiring it. In this model, learning is a process of connecting nodes of information, facilitated by digital tools such as online forums, social media and open educational resources. Throughout the 2000s and 2010s, growth in these areas was steadily increasing and learners were starting to access connectivist-based learning, though this was not prolific nor prevalent in schools, which saw technology as problematic, expensive and difficult to manage within schools; outside schools there existed a technological divide driven by deprivation. Some schools approached this issue of provision by reducing the number of fixed technology offerings (in the form of rooms full of PCs) and switching to a mobile technology offer in the form of alternative technology offers such as tablets, which was in keeping with advice to schools in the 2010s on how to navigate access to technology difficulties (Shea and Stockford, 2014).

COVID-19 AND THE RISE OF CONNECTIVISM

The COVID-19 pandemic significantly accelerated the adoption of connectivist learning environments. With schools and universities forced to shift rapidly to online platforms, teachers and students rapidly engaged in large-scale digital learning networks overnight despite widespread lack of knowledge or technological provision. Platforms such as Microsoft Teams™, Google Classroom™ and Zoom™ enabled real-time interaction, while social media groups and online forums became crucial spaces for knowledge-sharing and support. Schools had to make strategic decisions about which technology to use and based this on how connectivist learning takes place. This period saw a dramatic expansion of professional learning networks, with teachers collaborating across national and international borders to develop remote teaching strategies (Trust, 2020). The practice of teaching via connectivism became turbo-charged as teachers across the world developed their asynchronous and synchronous learning strategies, battling cameras that were turned off or students without access to the technology needed to engage in remote learning. In England, it rapidly became clear that laptops were in short supply in deprived households and that this was a barrier to connectivist learning. The government at the time invested in and distributed nearly 2 million laptops or tablet devices (Statista, 2024) to help remedy the deprivation of connectivist learning opportunities across the population of school-aged learners. This is known as a *first-order barrier* – simple access to technology.

Moreover, during and post the COVID-19 pandemic era, large-scale open learning environments such as MOOCs (massive open online courses) gained traction, building on the upskill in many people's ability to learn using the principles of connectivism. These platforms allowed for dynamic peer-to-peer interaction, where learners co-constructed knowledge through discussion forums, collaborative projects and shared digital resources. The COVID-19 pandemic reinforced the idea that learning occurs not just in formal institutions, but also through decentralised, networked communities (Bozkurt et al., 2020). However, traditional ideas about learning, especially those founded on face-to-face practice, have proved remarkably resilient due to *second-order barriers* (Bell and Barr, 2023). These barriers relate to knowledge and beliefs around technology, knowledge and expertise of connectivist learning principles, pedagogical beliefs about how the subject should be taught and school-wide policies which eschew connectivist pedagogical ideas in favour of traditional ideas.

Retrieval practice is a good example of this. Retrieval practice, which is a study method rather than a teaching pedagogy (it does not require a teacher), asks a student to sit cycles of retrieval study activities (e.g., recognition and recall questions) to generate the testing effect (Roediger and Karpicke, 2006; Roediger and Butler, 2011). No teaching is involved and as such the main learning theory is generally a behaviourist principle rather than cognitive science – *specific cued recall*. Cognitive science applies when the student experiences lower cognitive load during a task which requires strong recall.

Repeating the process in a cycle conditions the response of retrieving explicit semantic knowledge from the long-term memory into the short-term memory. The best way for this to take place is online and with an AI *large language model*. The AI model monitors the answers being given and ensures that new schemata is correctly being constructed, the right questions are being repeated (those where wrong answers are being given) and then students are actively constructing new knowledge into schemata, allowing for quick and accurate retrieval from long-term memory. However, rather than invest time and effort in developing this, schools are insisting on expensive teachers supervising (rather than teaching) the behaviourist principles of retrieval practice, often at the start of every lesson, undertaking time on the marking and, as Bates and Shea (2024) have found, spending further time re-teaching those items incorrectly retrieved. This shows how, even when the learning science of connectivism can deliver better outcomes, teachers and school leaders will be resilient to such ideas and stay resolute to traditional learning sciences.

CONCLUSION

Rigid or ideological adherence to teaching and learning policies based on a limited understanding of learning sciences can lead to exclusionary experiences for some students. Every student deserves to learn effectively and benefit from their teacher's comprehensive knowledge of learning sciences, along with the ability to adapt the learning experience to meet diverse needs.

PRACTICAL APPLICATION

Understanding the theoretical concepts of learning sciences is crucial for implementing these strategies in the classroom. However, considering how they can be practically applied is equally important.

CONSIDER THIS: GROUP LEARNING

Given that most teaching approaches blend ideas from multiple learning sciences, reflect on the concept of *group learning*.

Consider the following points:

- how behaviourism contributes to effective group work;

- how new knowledge is constructed through social interaction in group work;

- how cognitivism helps in understanding what constitutes effective group work;

- the pre-lesson and in-lesson adaptations you have made to ensure group work is a positive experience for all students;

- when group learning is not a good choice of pedagogy;

- what constitutes poor group learning.

SOCIAL CONSTRUCTIVISM IN PRACTICE

When thinking about implementing social constructivist concepts, group work often comes to mind. On the one hand, poorly managed group work can lead to unstructured chaos and frustration. Effective group work, on the other hand, can significantly enhance learning, especially in subjects where collaboration is essential, such as science, PE, music and drama.

For example, in a Year 7 science class, students might be paired to light a Bunsen burner. Pairing students with someone they feel comfortable with can help ease anxiety. Assigning roles such as 'fire starter' and 'Bunsen buddy' ensures that each student understands their responsibilities and the importance of their role, leading to a successful and safe learning experience.

In drama, groups can be carefully selected to include a mix of strong directors, performers and technicians. This allows students to play to their strengths while developing new skills. Assigning roles, even to those less willing to perform, such as a critic, ensures active involvement and constructive feedback.

BEHAVIOURISM AND CLASSROOM MANAGEMENT

Behaviourist principles can be effectively applied to manage classroom behaviour and reinforce positive actions. For instance, using a reward system to encourage participation and good behaviour during group work can be highly effective. In the lesson, a teacher might use a 'star chart' where students earn stars for positive behaviour, which can be exchanged for rewards. This system reinforces desired behaviours and provides clear expectations.

COGNITIVISM AND COGNITIVE LOAD MANAGEMENT

Cognitivist approaches, such as cognitive load theory, emphasise the importance of managing the cognitive load to optimise learning. Modelling is a practical tool that supports this theory. For example, in a class, a teacher might walk a group through a task in front of the rest of the students to model the process of successful group work. By replicating the exact process students will follow, including using the same resources, the teacher reduces cognitive load and helps students focus on each step.

CONNECTIVISM AND TECHNOLOGY INTEGRATION

Connectivism highlights the role of technology in learning. In a modern classroom, integrating technology can enhance learning experiences. For example, using online collaborative tools like Google Classroom allows students to work together on projects, share resources and provide feedback in real time. This approach not only supports collaborative learning, but also prepares students for a hyper-connected world.

BALANCING THEORY AND PRACTICE

While modelling and structured group work are effective, it is important to balance these with opportunities for independent practice. Over-reliance on modelling can lead to dependency, reducing students' ability to think independently and take risks. Teachers should provide opportunities for students to apply what they have learned independently, gradually increasing the complexity of tasks to build confidence and competence.

CHAPTER SUMMARY

There are numerous ways to practically apply learning theories in the classroom. The examples provided should help you start thinking about how to integrate these theories into your own subjects and teaching practices. Always reflect on and identify the intended purpose of the activity. Carefully consider the processes and structures you will put in place to ensure the activity is completed by the students as you intended. Understand and rationalise the purpose and effectiveness of the activity in ensuring positive outcomes and student progress.

A good starting point and professional practice when trying a new idea or activity in your classroom is to observe expert colleagues where this practice is already effectively embedded. This could be within your department if it is common practice, or in other departments if the strategy is more effectively used elsewhere. Simply opening a conversation with colleagues who frequently observe practice in your department or across the school, such as heads of subject or departments or teaching and learning leads, can help you identify teachers who excel at a given practice. This can provide guidance or highlight a gap in the skill set of the department or school, leading to opportunities for you to explore, research, develop and share good practice yourself.

The aim of this chapter was to stimulate your thinking about how the learning sciences have evolved over the past 50 years and how they can be synthesised and used in a blended way to support learning. We have explored a variety of learning theories that can and should inform our decisions when planning learning activities within our lessons. Whether planning new material from scratch or adapting existing resources, it is crucial to ensure an equitable experience for all pupils by making adaptations based on their responses.

A sound knowledge of the key tenets of the learning sciences enables us to support our pupils' learning effectively, confident that we are using the appropriate approach for each lesson. It is important to remember that our teaching approaches may vary depending on the class or even the time of day, and no two lessons will ever be identical. This flexibility is underpinned by good assessment for learning (AfL), where teachers use information about student achievement to adjust throughout the lesson (Wiliam, 2017). We remain vigilant to pupils' reactions and may change our approach based on their responses to questions and activities.

We have seen that there is a false dichotomy between the so-called 'traditional' approach to teaching, which includes direct instruction and behaviourist techniques, and the 'progressive' approaches, which incorporate social constructivist methods and a more dialogic way of teaching. In reality, there is a continuum of approaches that skilled teachers can choose from, depending on the situation, the individual pupils, the activity and the intended learning goals. Often, a period of behaviourist-driven direct instruction is necessary when teaching new knowledge or skills before pupils can form their own opinions and discuss possibilities in a social constructivist manner.

Activating pupils' pre-existing schema by linking new learning to similar experiences or related situations helps them commit new information to long-term memory and form new schema, while reducing the cognitive load required to grasp completely new concepts. Modelling by an expert and opportunities to practise new skills before moving on help consolidate learning, but this learning needs to be revisited several times before it becomes fully embedded and accessible to working memory.

Using a blend of learning sciences is likely to achieve optimal learning outcomes for our pupils. However, it is important to recognise that getting all the elements right is crucial; if one part is done poorly, the others will suffer. For example, the currently popular practice of *retrieval practice* at the beginning of lessons, based on theories of memory by Roediger and Butler (2011), suggests that revisiting learning from days or weeks earlier strengthens memory and reduces forgetting. However, if done poorly, this practice can activate inappropriate schemata (Piaget, 1952) for the upcoming lesson, causing extraneous cognitive load and confusion.

Schemas (or schemata) are abstract concepts that propose units of understanding, creating a web of complex relationships. New information attaches more easily to existing schemata, making it easier to remember. Importantly, new information will not attach to existing schemas if pupils are not already thinking about that schema when the information is introduced. This is why it is crucial to ensure that pupils are thinking about the relevant schema during retrieval practice.

Social constructivist learning, such as group work, is perhaps the most challenging form of pedagogy when it comes to blending learning sciences. Successful group work requires setting clear expectations and tightly controlling the process using behaviourist techniques. Pupils need some degree of direct instruction before working together, and the task must have clearly articulated roles, expected outcomes and pupil motivation to complete it to a high standard within the allocated time. Understanding social dynamics in collaborative learning is essential to ensure all pupils participate fully. Knowledge of motivation, self-confidence and self-efficacy theories helps teachers support pupils in collaborative activities.

Additionally, it is important to allow all pupils the opportunity to articulate their thinking during collaborative tasks to benefit equally from the positive impact of peer communication. Understanding dialogic approaches to teaching, as demonstrated by Alexander (2020), shows the power of talk to engage students, stimulate their thinking, advance their understanding and expand their ideas.

Using correct terms when discussing learning sciences and classroom practice helps develop pupils' understanding of *metacognition*. Metacognition involves learners using knowledge of the task, learning strategies and themselves to plan their learning, monitor their progress and evaluate the outcome.

REFLECTIVE QUESTIONS: CHAPTER 2

Reflect on your teaching experiences and consider the following questions.

- Can you identify a school or trust-wide rule or policy that was based on a particular learning science theory?
- In what situations did this rule or policy prove beneficial?
- Can you recall instances where the rule or policy was not suitable for an individual learner?
- Did you have the autonomy to modify or disregard the rule to make it more inclusive?
- Do you have an example of a positive outcome resulting from a teacher's inclusive approach?
- Do you have an example of a student's learning experience being negatively impacted by strict adherence to a narrow rule or policy?

FURTHER READING

ITTECF 4.9 Paired and group activities can increase pupil success, but to work together effectively pupils need guidance, support and practice.

Kirschner, P., Sweller, J., Kirschner, F. and Zambrano, J. (2018). From cognitive load theory to collaborative cognitive load theory. *International Journal of Computer-Supported Collaborative Learning*, *13*(2), 213–33. Available at: https://doi.org/10.1007/s11412-018-9277-y

Based on the principles in Kirschner et al.'s paper, effective group work relies on minimising wasted mental effort, or extraneous cognitive load. This is achieved by creating an environment where a student's cognitive load is optimal for constructing new knowledge. Teachers should therefore design group tasks with these principles in mind. One key strategy is to assign specific roles to students, which helps to reduce the cognitive load associated with communication and coordination. Additionally, tasks should be carefully structured into manageable steps to prevent students from feeling overwhelmed. By ensuring that students have the necessary foundational knowledge before they begin and by monitoring groups to provide timely guidance, teachers can transform collaborative activities into powerful learning experiences.

═══ REFERENCES ═══

Alexander, R. (2020). *A Dialogic Teaching Companion*. London: Routledge.

Baddeley, A. D. (2000). The episodic buffer: a new component of working memory? *Trends in Cognitive Sciences, 4*(11), 417–23.

Bates, G. and Shea, J. (2024). Retrieval practice in the wild. *Mind, Brain and Education, 18*(3), 211–381.

Bell, E. and Barr, D. (2023). Barriers to technology integration in the A-level history classroom in Northern Ireland. *Irish Educational Studies, 43*(4), 1227–48.

Bozkurt, A., ... and Bond, M. (2020). A global outlook to the interruption of education due to COVID-19 pandemic: navigating in a time of uncertainty and crisis. *Asian Journal of Distance Education, 15*(1), 1–126.

Bruner, J. S. (1960). *The Process of Education*. Cambridge, MA: Harvard University Press.

Clark, R. C. and Mayer, R. E. (2016). *E-learning and the Science of Instruction: Proven Guidelines for Consumers and Designers of Multimedia Learning*. Hoboken, NJ: John Wiley & Sons.

Department for Education (DfE) (2013). *Teachers' Standards*. London: DfE.

Downes, S. (2008). An introduction to connective knowledge. In T. Hug (ed.), *Media, Knowledge and Education: Exploring New Spaces, Relations and Dynamics in Digital Media Ecologies*. Innsbruck: Innsbruck University Press.

Gibb, N. (2017a). *The Evidence in Favour of Teacher-Led Instruction*. Available at: www.gov.uk/government/speeches/nick-gibb-the-evidence-in-favour-of-teacher-led-instruction. Accessed 2 June 2020.

Gibb, N. (2017b). *The Importance of Knowledge-Based Education*. Available at: www.gov.uk/government/speeches/nick-gibb-the-importance-of-knowledge-based-education. Accessed 2 June 2020.

Gove, M. (2012). *Letter from Secretary of State for Education to Tim Oates of the Expert Review Panel*. Available at: http://data.parliament.uk/DepositedPapers/Files/DEP2012-0902/LetterfromSoStoTimOates.pdf. Accessed 2 June 2020.

Hirsch, E. D. (1987). *Cultural Literacy: What Every American Needs to Know*. Boston, MA: Houghton Mifflin.

Hirsch, E. D. (1996). *The Schools We Need and Why We Don't Have Them*. New York: Doubleday.

Hirsch, E. D. (2006). *The Knowledge Deficit: Closing the Shocking Education Gap*. Boston, MA: Houghton Mifflin.

Kirschner, P., Sweller, J., Kirschner, F. and Zambrano, J. (2018). From cognitive load theory to collaborative cognitive load theory. *International Journal of Computer-Supported Collaborative Learning*, *13*(2), 213–33. Available at: https://doi.org/10.1007/s11412-018-9277-y

Lave, J. and Wenger, E. (1991). *Situated Learning: Legitimate Peripheral Participation*. Cambridge: Cambridge University Press.

Marsh, C. J. (2017). *Curriculum: The Strategic Management of Learning*. London: Routledge.

Piaget, J. (1952). *The Origins of Intelligence in Children*. Madison, CT: International Universities Press.

Roediger, H. L. and Butler, A. C. (2011). The critical role of retrieval practice in long-term retention. *Trends in Cognitive Sciences*, *15*(1), 20–7.

Roediger, H. L. and Karpicke, J. D. (2006). Test-enhanced learning: taking memory tests improves long-term retention. *Psychological Science*, *17*(3), 249–55.

Shea, J. (2019). The hidden voice of pre-service teachers in their private social media interactions. In J. Wearmouth and A. Goodwyn (eds), *Pupil, Teacher and Student Voice in Educational Institutions: Values, Opinions, Beliefs and Perspectives*. London: Routledge.

Shea, J. and Stockford, A. (2014). *The Mobile Technology Offer*. Available at: www.gov.uk/government/publications/the-mobile-technology-offer. Accessed 19 February 2025.

Siemens, G. (2005). Connectivism: a learning theory for the digital age. *International Journal of Instructional Technology and Distance Learning*, *2*(1), 3–10.

Skinner, B. F. (1953). *Science and Human Behavior*. New York: Macmillan.

Statista (2024). *Educational Digital Devices Delivered by UK Government*. Available at: www.statista.com/statistics/1263494/educational-digital-devices-delivered-by-uk-government/. Accessed 19 February 2025.

Sweller, J., van Merriënboer, J. J. G. and Paas, F. (2019). Cognitive architecture and instructional design: 20 years later. *Educational Psychology Review*, *31*(2), 261–92.

Trust, T. (2020). The COVID-19 transition: teachers' digital learning communities as a support system during emergency remote teaching. *Journal of Technology and Teacher Education*, *28*(2), 151–9.

Tversky, A. and Kahneman, D. (1992). Advances in prospect theory: cumulative representation of uncertainty. *Journal of Risk and Uncertainty*, *5*(4), 297–323.

Vygotsky, L. S. (1978). *Mind in Society: The Development of Higher Psychological Processes*. Cambridge, MA: Harvard University Press.

Wenger, E. (1998). *Communities of Practice: Learning, Meaning, and Identity*. Cambridge: Cambridge University Press.

Wiliam, D. (2017). Assessment for learning: why it works and what it means for practice. *REL Journal*, *8*(3), 1–25.

Willingham, D. T. (2017). A mental model of the learner: teaching the basic science of educational psychology to future teachers. *Mind, Brain, and Education, 11*(4), 166–75.

Young, M. F. D. (2010). *The Curriculum of the Future: From the New Sociology of Education to a Critical Realist Approach to Curriculum Theory.* London: Routledge.

Young, M. F. D. (2011). The return of subjects: a sociological perspective on the UK coalition government's approach to the 14–19 *curriculum.* Curriculum Journal, *22*(3), 265–78.

3

THE LEARNING SCIENCES

BLENDED OR ISOLATED IN THE CLASSROOM TODAY?

LEARNING OUTCOMES

By reading this chapter you will develop:

- An understanding of the rise of schools that specifically focus on an isolated approach of a singular learning theory
- Consideration of the good and problematic practices from an isolated approach to learning theories in schools
- Consideration of the good and problematic practices from a blended approach to learning theories in schools

INITIAL TEACHER TRAINING AND EARLY CAREER FRAMEWORK (ITTECF)

The key reading from the ITTECF that is to be explored within this chapter is:

Kirschner, P., Sweller, J., Kirschner, F. and Zambrano, J. (2018). From cognitive load theory to collaborative cognitive load theory. *International Journal of Computer-Supported Collaborative Learning, 13*(2), 213–33. https://doi.org/10.1007/s11412-018-9277-y

INTRODUCTION

Historically, many schools and educational programmes have adopted a singular, isolated approach to teaching and learning, often rooted in one dominant learning theory. This has manifested in 'knowledge-rich' schools, for instance, which are heavily influenced by cognitive science, prioritising explicit instruction and the acquisition of core knowledge. Conversely, other institutions advocate for more progressive, student-centred pedagogies, often drawing from social constructivist principles. This chapter will explore the efficacy of these isolated approaches, analysing their strengths and limitations. Furthermore, this chapter will argue for the necessity of a blended approach, one that strategically integrates insights from various learning sciences to create a more robust and effective pedagogical model. Specifically, we will focus on the work of Kirschner et al. (2018), who present a compelling argument for blending a cognitive approach with collaborative methodologies, leading to the development of *collaborative cognitive load theory* (CCLT).

THE PITFALLS OF PEDAGOGICAL TRIBALISM

When exploring the limitations of isolated approaches you will find the history of educational theory is, in many ways, a story of 'pedagogical tribalism' where proponents of different learning sciences have often been at odds. For decades, the field has seen a persistent, and at times acrimonious, divide between rival schools of thought. On one side, you will have seen the rise of cognitivism, which, in its more dogmatic forms, has a tendency to eschew social constructivism. This is evident in the push for explicit instruction and individual, silent work, driven by the desire to minimise extraneous cognitive load. The core belief here is that the most efficient way to transfer knowledge is directly from you to your students, and that group work or discovery learning can introduce unnecessary distractions and cognitive burdens that hinder learning (Kirschner et al., 2006).

On the other side, constructivists, especially social constructivists, have often lamented the march of direct instruction, which they associate with the behaviourist traditions of rote learning and memorisation. Their argument is that knowledge is not a commodity to be transferred, but is actively constructed by the learner through their interaction with their environment and with others (Piaget, 1972). From this perspective, a reliance on direct instruction is seen as a passive and ineffective form of learning that fails to develop deep understanding and critical thinking skills. This is a crucial point of contention, as it forces you to choose between pedagogical philosophies rather than drawing from the best of both.

DIGITAL AMPLIFICATION OF THE DIVIDE: CONNECTIVISM AND THE CONTEMPORARY TEACHER

Today's digital landscape further highlights the limitations of isolated approaches by dangerously amplifying pedagogical tribalism. The advent of online collectivism, facilitated by social media and professional forums, has profoundly changed how teachers learn. This new reality is underpinned by the principles of connectivism (Siemens, 2005), which posits that learning is a process of connecting specialised information nodes or sources. As a teacher, you now have unprecedented access to a global network of peers, research papers, blog posts and resources, allowing you to build your own *personal learning network* (PLN). This has democratised professional development, moving it beyond traditional in-school training and into a dynamic, ongoing dialogue. You might learn a new technique by following a teacher on X, formerly Twitter, or gain a deeper understanding of a concept by joining a subject-specific Facebook™ group. This aligns with the work of Lave and Wenger (1991) on communities of practice, where you learn through active participation in a social context, moving from a novice to a more experienced member.

However, the algorithms that govern social media platforms tend to create echo chambers, where you are primarily exposed to content and opinions that already align with your own. For a teacher who is a staunch cognitivist, their feed will be filled with posts from others advocating for explicit instruction while negatively critiquing constructivist approaches. Conversely, a constructivist teacher's digital world will be dominated by content celebrating discovery learning and lamenting the direct instruction and rote learning that they see as stifling creativity. This self-reinforcing cycle hardens philosophical stances and makes it more difficult for you to engage in a nuanced dialogue with those who hold different views. The tribalism that once existed in academic journals is now played out in real-time, bite-sized conflicts on public platforms, further cementing the false dichotomy between rival learning theories.

This theoretical tribalism has created a false dichotomy in education, where you and your school leaders can feel pressured to favour one approach over another. However, this is a flawed premise. As this book has repeatedly said, the most effective teaching and learning does not come from a single theory but from a strategic blend of them. The focus of this chapter is to break down these theoretical walls, showing you how insights from different learning sciences can be integrated to create a more powerful pedagogical model. It is through this blended approach, for instance, that the cognitive principles of managing working memory can be reconciled with the social benefits of collaborative learning.

LEARNING SCIENCES: BLENDED OR ISOLATED IN THE CLASSROOM TODAY?

The core idea of this chapter is that a singular, dogmatic adherence or preference to one learning theory can be limiting to you, your students and their success trajectories throughout their lives. It is crucial to recognise that your own teaching practice is already a blend of various theories. It is important to reflect on how your school's or trust's policies might be founded on favouring a singular idea – for example, a policy that mandates only explicit, teacher-led instruction in all lessons may be rooted in a purely cognitive science approach, prioritising the reduction of extraneous cognitive load through direct teaching. In contrast, a policy that requires all learning to be project-based and student-led may be based solely on constructivist principles, emphasising active knowledge construction over passive reception. It is crucial for you to consider the theoretical underpinnings of your school's practices and to be able to identify both their strengths and their potential drawbacks. While a school might endorse a specific pedagogical ideology, the reality of a single lesson often requires a combination of different approaches.

A school or trust-wide rule may be founded upon an idea from a specific learning theory. For example, a policy pushing for lots of silent, individual work, with an emphasis on students working from a trust- or teacher-authored workbook or official textbook, is often rooted in cognitive load theory, with the intention of minimising social interaction and, therefore, extraneous cognitive load. Conversely, a policy that requires a certain percentage of the curriculum to be delivered through group projects or collaborative activities is typically an application of constructivist or social learning theories, promoting peer-to-peer learning and active knowledge construction.

Given that most teaching approaches already blend ideas from multiple learning sciences, you should reflect on your own practice and consider how you can be more intentional about it. Think about how a blended approach changes your role from that of a knowledge transmitter or a facilitator of learning to one where you consider each context, the needs of the students and the best approach for the occasion.

PRACTICAL APPLICATION

CONSIDER THIS: WHEN AN APPROACH DIDN'T WORK

- Consider a time when a purely explicit or purely student-led approach did not work. For instance, an overly complex topic may have been too difficult for your students to grasp through discovery alone, or a long, silent task may have disengaged some students who benefit from collaboration.

- You should also reflect on how technology facilitates a blended approach. For example, a digital tool can provide a scaffold (cognitivism) while allowing for collaborative, project-based work (constructivism).

To demonstrate the efficacy of a blended approach, the principles of collaborative cognitive load theory can be applied in a classroom to enhance both individual and group learning. One practical case study involves a science teacher implementing a complex problem-solving task. Instead of your students working individually on a difficult physics problem using a workbook, they are placed in small, carefully composed groups. You can use a blended approach, first providing a short period of explicit instruction to introduce the core concepts and reduce intrinsic cognitive load (Kirschner et al., 2006). Your students then work collaboratively to solve the problem with each member having a specific role and specific tasks related to their unique role. During this phase, you circulate, providing specific, targeted support only when needed. This acts as a scaffold, helping to reduce extraneous cognitive load and prevent frustration. The group setting and guidance from you allows your students to distribute the cognitive effort, with each member contributing their unique knowledge and perspective. This approach not only helps your students to arrive at a solution, but also develops their collaborative and communication skills.

Another example could be in a humanities lesson where a history teacher could apply CCLT by having students work in pairs to analyse a primary source document that contains complex, archaic language. You first provide an explicit key to the text, explaining key terms and historical context to reduce the initial cognitive load. The students then work in pairs to decipher the text, with one student reading a section and the other explaining it in their own words. This collaborative process allows them to share the cognitive burden and discuss their interpretations, leading to a more profound understanding than if they were working alone. The pair's discussion and negotiation of meaning form a powerful feedback loop that reinforces learning and aids in the transfer to long-term memory.

CHAPTER SUMMARY

This chapter has explored the notion that teaching and learning is not a matter of *either/or* when it comes to learning theories. Instead, it is an *and* approach, where a thoughtful and strategic blend of ideas from different learning sciences can lead to a more powerful and effective pedagogical model. The concept of CCLT, as presented by Kirschner et al. (2018), provides a clear example of how insights from cognitivism can be combined with those from social learning theories to create a framework that enhances learning outcomes. It challenges the idea that explicit, teacher-led instruction and student-led, collaborative work must be in opposition. Instead, they can be seen as two essential components of a cohesive learning experience. The real power of this approach lies in its ability to support your students in tackling more complex tasks than they could manage alone, while also developing the crucial skills of teamwork and communication.

Arguing for the necessity of a blended approach, this chapter has explored the benefits of such an approach to learning, arguing against the limitations of over reliance on a single learning theory in a school or trust's policies and CPD offer. It has focused on CCLT as a powerful example of how insights from different learning sciences can be integrated to create a more effective pedagogical model. We have seen that a well-structured blended approach, which combines explicit instruction with collaborative tasks, can significantly reduce the cognitive load on individual learners, allowing them to tackle more complex problems and transition information more effectively to long-term memory. However, this approach requires careful planning and a deep understanding of the *transactional costs* of collaboration. The conclusion is clear: the most effective teaching practice is not one that adheres strictly to a single theory, but one that thoughtfully and strategically blends ideas from a variety of learning sciences to meet the diverse needs of your students in the modern classroom.

REFLECTIVE QUESTIONS: CHAPTER 3

Think about the idea that most approaches to teaching and learning blend ideas from multiple learning sciences. Reflect on these questions.

- How you ensure your students know how to work with each other within your subject during socially constructivist tasks using behaviourist principles?

- When you want students to complete work independently and in silence, can they undertake this behaviour easily or do they struggle?

- When you set homework that requires independent knowledge acquisition, do your students access reliable and authentic sources of information or do they struggle to identify and discern suitable sources?

— FURTHER READING —

ITTECF 4.10 How pupils are grouped is also important; care should be taken to monitor the impact of groupings on pupil attainment, behaviour and motivation.

Kirschner, P., Sweller, J., Kirschner, F. and Zambrano, J. (2018). From cognitive load theory to collaborative cognitive load theory. *International Journal of Computer-Supported Collaborative Learning, 13*(2), 213–33. https://doi.org/10.1007/s11412-018-9277-y

This paper by Kirschner et al. reviews the popular cognitive load theory (CLT) that underpins the learning theory of cognitivism and considers the benefits of blending it with strategies and approaches from other learning theories – in particular, constructivism and connectivism – to introduce the concept of collaborative cognitive load theory (CCLT), explaining that transition to long-term memory is most effective when unnecessary cognitive load is minimised.

It then moves on to discuss the benefits of collaboration in this process, with the concept that when multiple learners share cognitive effort towards a common goal it has the potential to reduce individual cognitive load – the key advantages being that this approach allows learners to process more complex tasks that may exceed an individual's cognitive limits, as well as being able to gain new knowledge through peer interaction to refine their own understanding.

This all sounds greatly beneficial to improve development of long-term memory, until the transactional costs of communication, coordination and, in some cases, conflict resolutions are considered; the practice may become ineffective if these costs begin to outweigh the benefits on reduced cognitive load. It may also become more limited if this type of learning is something they are not familiar with and do not have the metacognitive skills to approach effectively.

Therefore, the authors provide the following points for consideration when implementing CCLT, taken from various core learning theories. Where a task is too complex for an individual working memory it can be undertaken in conjunction with appropriate support to reduce extraneous cognitive load by guiding learning through effective teamwork. This may include the consideration by the teacher of the most efficient group sizes, composition (novices vs experts) and roles within the groups to optimise the number of transactions required for the best cognitive outcome. Prior experience in completing similar tasks and working collaboratively means that knowledge levels of the individuals across a group are appropriate to ensure the task does not become too overwhelming or the collaboration redundant.

In conclusion, the key takeaway for this chapter is that though collaboration can provide many benefits, including the reduction of individual cognitive load, it must be structured carefully, fully considering the factors that may have a negative effect on the outcome and ensuring the right balance to enhance collective cognition and the learning process as a whole.

— REFERENCES —

Kirschner, P. A., Sweller, J. and Clark, R. E. (2006). Why minimal guidance during instruction does not work: an analysis of the failure of constructivist, discovery, problem-based, experiential, and inquiry-based teaching. *Educational Psychologist, 41*(2), 75–86.

Lave, J. and Wenger, E. (1991). *Situated Learning: Legitimate Peripheral Participation.* Cambridge: Cambridge University Press.

Piaget, J. (1972). *The Psychology of the Child.* New York: Basic Books.

Siemens, G. (2005). Connectivism: a learning theory for the digital age. *International Journal of Instructional Technology and Distance Learning,* 2(1).

PART 2

4
BEHAVIOURISM

LEARNING OUTCOMES

By reading this chapter you will develop:

- An understanding of the core research and theories underpinning behaviourism
- An understanding of some of the approaches to incorporating behaviourist strategies into teaching practice
- An understanding of some of the risks and limitations of the behaviourist approach

INITIAL TEACHER TRAINING AND EARLY CAREER FRAMEWORK (ITTECF)

The key reading from the ITTECF that is to be explored within this chapter is:

Lazowski, R. A. and Hulleman, C. S. (2016). Motivation interventions in education: a meta-analytic review. *Review of Educational Research, 86*(2), 602–40. https://doi.org/10.3102/003465 4315617832

INTRODUCTION

The theory of behaviourism posits that behaviour is a passive conditioning in response to external environmental stimuli, a concept famously observed in Pavlov's classical conditioning experiments (1927). John B. Watson (1930) further built upon these origins, setting out assumptions that all behaviours are learned from the environment through classical conditioning and association to a stimulus. This chapter will explore the core theories underpinning behaviourism, including Skinner's operant conditioning (1938) and its application in classroom management through positive and negative reinforcement, as well as punishment. Furthermore, this chapter will examine the strengths, limitations and potential risks of behaviourist approaches, including their use in contemporary strategies like those found in Lemov's *Teach Like a Champion* (2015), and consider how behaviourism can be effectively blended with other learning sciences.

Drawing from the foundational principles of Pavlov's (1927) and Watson's (1913) work, this process of passive conditioning is evident in numerous real-life examples. For instance, a toddler can learn emotions, behaviours and language by observing external stimuli in their environment, or individuals may develop phobias and irrational fears from negative experiences. These foundational ideas consequently inform the basic approach to implementing behaviourism within the classroom. For example, if a clear stimulus, such as a countdown, is consistently and repeatedly paired with a desired response, like students stopping their current activity and focusing on the teacher, pupils will, over time, associate the two and respond accordingly.

Skinner (1957) later argued that learning is an active process and occurs through operant conditioning, building on the work of Thorndike's (1898) *law of effect.* Theorising that the views of classical conditioning were too simplistic for the complexity of human behaviour, Skinner used animals such as rats and pigeons in his study. They were placed in boxes, known as operant conditioning chambers, where they were either rewarded or punished for engaging in certain behaviours, such as lever pressing (rats) or key pecking (pigeons). By pressing one leaver or key the animal was rewarded with food; when pressing another they were punished by an electric shock through an electric grid in the base of the chamber. The animals learned over time which one provided the food (a reward) and which one the shock (a punishment) and were seen to increase frequency of the action that provided the reward and decrease the frequency of the action the provided the punishment. This brought in the idea of *reinforcement* into the process of conditioning, where a behaviour that elicits a positive outcome or reward is more like to be repeated whereas a behaviour that brings a negative outcome, or punishment will occur less frequently.

Again, if we apply this to the previous example of the countdown and becoming silent, if the students followed the expected response and became focused on the teacher and received a positive reward, such as praise or a 'token' (such as a merit or house point in a reward system), over time they would be more likely to associate the two and respond in that way. If a negative reinforcement (such as ignoring the behaviour) or a punishment (such as being told off, or a demerit in a reward system) was given for not following the expectations, they would associate the two and over time are likely to reduce the negative behaviour.

KEY PRINCIPLES OF BEHAVIOURISM

The use of positive reinforcement has been seen to foster a sense of accomplishment and self-confidence within students as well promoting a strong work ethic and moral compass, as discussed by Timbrell (2024) in an article for *Educater* [sic] upon reviewing research from studies in Chinese schools. In addition, Chinese students also reported better teacher–student interactions from the use of positive reinforcement.

Negative reinforcement is the idea of removing the negative condition or stimulus to reinforce a positive behaviour outcome. For example, if you a PE teacher and you are trying to encourage students to be respectful to one another but one throws a ball at the other, then the removal of the ball is a negative reinforcement as you are encouraging more respectful behaviour by removing the negative stimulus – in this case the ball. Therefore, negative reinforcement can become a powerful tool if it follows three key steps.

- *Immediacy*: the longer between the unacceptable behaviour and the negative reinforcement, the less impactful it will be as the student might begin to believe the behaviour is acceptable.

- *Frequency*: it is important to reinforce the positive behaviour by using the negative reinforcement every time the condition or stimulus arises.

- *Consistency*: if you are not consistent, the student will be unsure of the expectations when they exhibit poor behaviour and therefore will be more likely to repeat it.

It is also important to note that negative reinforcement is different to punishment in operant conditioning. Negative reinforcement encourages an increase in behaviour whereas punishment's aim is to decrease a behaviour by bringing an unpleasant consequence after the behaviour has already occurred to decrease the chance of it occurring again – for example, giving a student who does not follow your expectations and is talking too much a detention at break time is a punishment as you are removing the positive consequence after the behaviour has occurred (Dozier et al., 2019). Punishment is intended to be an aversive stimulus to decrease the likelihood of the behaviour being repeated, whereas negative reinforcement removes the aversive stimulus to increase the likelihood of a behaviour being repeated.

THE FURTHER DEVELOPMENT OF BEHAVIOURISM

It was noted by Clore and Collin (1988) in a study by Dad et al. (2010) that negative reinforcement is most effective when used sparingly and only for behaviours that are considered genuinely undesirable. If used too frequently or for minor issues it will become ineffective. Additionally, the aversive stimulus must be something the student cares about, if they do not care about detention, then the threat of a detention is unlikely to sway them from the negative behaviour. Dad et al. (2010) goes on to argue that punishment (and to an extent negative reinforcement) should only be used as a 'last resort' after other methods of behavioural change have failed. Therefore, negative reinforcement should only really be used to complement or further support positive reinforcement which tends to have a higher continuous success rate – but again only if the reward is something the student cares about.

Lemov's (2015) *Teach Like a Champion* is a popular behaviour strategy implemented by many schools where the setting and building, maintaining high expectations, creating strong classroom culture and building character and trust underpin the core methods used by Lemov in his suggested approach. These include techniques like, *no opt out*, where students are encouraged to have a go and 'I don't know' is not accepted, along with *right is right* (no half answers) and *no apologies*. These are built upon with the ideas of *explicit instruction* and that students conform *100 per cent* of the time to teachers' expectations, paired with a *no warning* approach when providing consequences. This is combined with a warm and strict approach to behaviour management, with emotional consistency from the teacher along with ideas like the *J factor* (which aims to bring the joy to the student experience) and *precise praise*. Through these techniques the combination and use of positive and negative reinforcement can be clearly seen. However, the strict zero-tolerance approach to teaching and expectations in the classroom outlined by Lemov has, over the years, been met with various criticisms, particularly the notion that all students and their learning are treated the same without consideration of individual needs. This often leads to modified or reduced versions being utilised in schools. Lemov, in an interview with *Schools Week* in 2021 (Coughlan, 2021), responded to this by explaining he felt that often techniques like SLANT (sit up, listen, ask and answer questions, nod your head, track the teacher), which are discussed further in Chapter 8, were misunderstood and that teachers did not think enough about the *why* and *how*. He goes on to discuss the *power of habits* for students with SEND and how this can be implemented in his approach. This is a debate that appears to be ongoing about the merit and effectiveness of strict behaviourist approach.

CRITICISMS OF BEHAVIOURISM

Further criticism to the behaviourist approach in general should be considered, such as the idea that the approach only values learning, resulting in modified behaviour through cause and effect where learning takes place within a complex set of criteria. It also theorises that learning is passive, and that the teacher is in control of the learning based on the environment they create. This removes the agency of students to engage meaningfully in their own learning, as well as the accountability of the underlying reason and internal process that led to the behaviour in the first place. Consequently, we might ask whether behaviourism should be used more to motivate students to engage with their learning rather than as a learning method itself – which could lead to it being paired with other learning theories such as social cognitive theory and constructionism to gain the benefits of the combined approach when applied in the classroom.

CONCLUSION: BEHAVIOURISM

Behaviourism suggests that providing the correct environment along with repetition of skills and knowledge task will lead to learning. It indicates that the teacher has a core responsibility to provide students with knowledge and that creating the correct conditions and responses to stimuli will allow this to happen effectively.

PRACTICAL APPLICATION

Behaviourist approaches are best implemented in a clearly routine approach with frequency, consistency and immediacy at the core of this. It seems only logical to consider practical applications where these types of routines can most easily be embedded into daily practice to give opportunities for effective impact.

CONSIDER THIS: YOUR OWN PRACTICE

Consider your own practice and reflect on how you have used behaviourism within your teaching.

- Do you have an anecdote or example of where you have seen effective use of positive or negative reinforcement? Can you explain how this was effective?

- Do you have an anecdote or example of where you have seen an ineffective use of positive or negative reinforcement? Can you explain why this was ineffective?

PROMPT AND POSITIVE STARTS

A prompt start to a lesson sets high expectations from the beginning; students enter the classroom and immediately know this is a space for learning and engaging in that learning. Thus, creating a clear routine for start of lesson is a very effective strategy to help create the right learning environment from the word go. Standing and greeting students at the door, sometimes known as 'one foot in, one foot out' not only starts the lesson with a positive teacher–student interaction such as a 'good morning' or 'are we ready to learn', showing the teacher has equal respect for all students, it also provides opportunities to set high expectations quickly before the start of the lesson, such as checking and correcting uniform before they enter the room or giving clear instructions such as handing out books or starting do now tasks promptly. Standing at the door also allows you to monitor both inside the classroom and the corridor, offer praise, reminders or corrections to those who warrant it in the room while also encouraging those in the corridor to enter the learning space promptly. All these micro-interactions quickly and effectively set your expectations to all students; by repeating this process every lesson the students will become accustomed to the expectations and the number of reminders required should decrease, allowing more time to focus on positive interactions and reinforcement using strategies such as precise praise.

PRECISE PRAISE

Precise praise is exactly as it sounds, using specific comments that reinforce both positive behaviour and academic actions, and can be used in numerous ways. For instance, it can reinforce actions chosen by students such as work ethic, improving on previous errors or following steps and showing resilience when solving a problem. This creates positive reinforcement for the student(s) you are praising, therefore they are encouraged to continue the action. The praise needs to be precise, so be specific when stating what has earned the student praise; it should be given when students have exceeded expectations, not just met them. For example, an acknowledgement may be 'Thank you for getting your books out and starting the do now task'; this is an expectation that all students should do in your lesson and therefore does not require positive praise. However, if a student provides a good, detailed answer in a class discussion they can be given precise praise such as, 'Thank you, I really liked how you linked [concept x] to [concept y] in your answer', or 'Well done, you gave a great explanation to your reasoning in that answer'. It is clear in these statements what specifically the student is being praised for, encouraging that student and others to endeavour to do similar. Praise does not always need to be in front of the whole class; some students may find it more rewarding when the teacher takes the time to praise them one-to-one in a quite conversation or in a small group. Additionally, the sharing of good class work with an explanation of why it is good (using a visualiser) also promotes positive reinforcement without necessarily identifying the specific student – especially when some students may be more reluctant to be called out in front of their peers, even if in a positive way. This can also be achieved with grouped praise such as 'Thank you everyone who has put their pens down and is actively listening to me for their next instructions' – which precisely praises those who are being successful without singling out students who may find that uncomfortable, as well as addressing the expected behaviour for all students not currently following it. However, it is crucial to ensure that this type of praise is genuine and not sarcastic or overused as these will decrease the effectiveness and validity of the praise.

TRANSITIONS

Another part of a lesson where setting and maintaining high expectations is crucial is during transitions between learning episodes. Often teachers will implement a simple 3–2–1 countdown to signal this. Paring the countdown with specific instructions gives clearer expectations and opportunities for positive and negative reinforcement. For example, '3. Everybody put your pens down. 2. Finish your conversations. 1. And all eyes and ears on me' gives explicit instructions and expectations for student to follow; praise can then be used for those who follow and negative reinforcement for those who don't, such as, 'If you continue to talk when I have asked for conversations to finish then I will have to move your seats away from those who might distract you.' This removes the negative stimulus (the person they are chatting too), reinforcing the positive behaviour of not talking when they have been asked to stop.

USING THE SCHOOL'S BEHAVIOUR POLICY

Along with all the in-classroom strategies that an individual teacher can implement to positive or negatively reinforce behaviour most if not all schools will have a behaviour policy seating in the concepts of behaviourism. It will often start with positive or negative reinforcement then escalate to a form of punishment, with the level of punishment increasing if students proceed to not meet expectations after each level prior. This is often coupled with restorative strategies to provide opportunities to clarify incorrect behaviours and reinforce correct behaviours. This highlights that clarity is key for students, especially when introducing negative reinforcement or punishment. The students need to be clear on exactly what they have done wrong, what will happen if they continue and how they can rectify this in the future to avoid this. Using a script such as 'You were doing "X"; if you continue this "Y" will happen; to avoid this you need to do "Z"' – where 'X' is the incorrect behaviour, 'Y' is the negative reinforcement or punishment and 'Z' is the modified correct behaviour – ensures clarity, so the student is fully aware of the expectations on them and the consequences if they do not meet them. Following this with asking them if they understand or to repeat back what they need to do or what will happen if they don't will also support the reinforcement further.

CONCLUSION

As you can see with the example of application outlined above, you could effectively include behaviourism strategies in your lessons in various ways and at various points alongside other learning theories and strategies to ensure an effective and purposeful classroom environment that is focused on motivated learning. The applications above are only a fraction of the possible uses; it is up to you as the teacher to find the strategies that work best for your classroom environment, ensuring that you follow the three core implementation principles of immediacy, frequency and consistency. Frequent reflection on the effectiveness and purpose of the strategy and careful consideration of the processes and structure you are going to put in place will ensure the strategy meets the needs of you, as the teacher, and the class. Whenever you want to implement a new strategy, especially when it comes to behaviourist approaches, good professional practice is to observe expert others who have already effectively implemented these theories into their practice, focusing particular attention on their use of positive and negative reinforcement in a variety of situations. These observations can be in department, if is it is already common practice, or out of department if it is known that that strategy is more effectively embedded elsewhere. Start by opening a conversation with colleagues whose role is to more frequently observe practice in your department or across the school, such as heads of subject or departments or behaviour leads; this will help you identify teachers who excel at a given practice and provide the best observation experiences.

CONSIDER THIS: A TOOL FOR IMPROVING STUDENT ENGAGEMENT

Consider behaviourism more as a tool for improving student engagement and motivation over direct learning. In reflecting on this, think about:

- how positive reinforcement can be used effectively in the classroom;

- whether punishment can effectively motivate students to engage;

- how and when you would use negative reinforcement over positive reinforcement;

- whether it is possible to pre-plan behaviourist strategies for a lesson prior to its delivery.

CHAPTER SUMMARY

This chapter began with an introduction to the behaviourist approach, discussing the works of key practitioners such as Pavlov and Skinner, introducing the concept of classical and operant conditioning as a foundation for behaviourism in the classroom. It went on to explore the concepts of positive and negative reinforcement and punishment and how these can be powerful tools in delivering effective behaviourism strategies in the classroom if used correctly, following the three core ideas of immediacy, frequency and consistency. There was also discussion on when to use negative reinforcement or punishment over positive reinforcement and a consideration of the impacts this might have on the students and the learning environment – highlighting that it is important to get the balance right.

The conversation was then moved on to an exploration of more modern approaches to behaviourism in the classroom through Lemov's (2015) *Teach Like a Champion*. Some of the techniques championed by Lemov were highlighted, with reflection on how they support a behaviourist approach – for example, no opt out, right is right and no apologies –strongly leaning into a zero-tolerance behaviourist classroom environment. These were also paired with techniques like warm and strict and the J factor which provide some balance, opportunities to build mutual respect between teachers and pupils and spark excitement within student learning, moving away from the zero-tolerance approach and providing more consideration to the student as a complex learner with a variety of needs.

This makes clear the limitations of behaviourism as the sole tool for learning in the classroom as criticisms were highlighted – particularly the ideas that this approach theorises that learning is passive and removes agency from students to engage, as well as removing accountability. As a consequence, it is considered move effective when paired with tools and strategies from other learning theories to achieve an optimum learning environment.

The suggested practical applications and reflections take into account not only the core theoretical approaches, but also the realistic nature of where behaviourism is beneficial and limited in the classroom environment; it asks you, the reader, to consider this carefully and encourages your to reflect on it before implementing it in your classrooms to ensure that the approaches you use are effective and do not risk adverse effects.

REFLECTIVE QUESTIONS: CHAPTER 4

Reflect on some of the classes you have taught within the schools you have worked as a teacher and ask yourself some reflective questions as follows.

Review your school's behaviour policy and consider how this is underpinned by or deviated from the strategies suggested by the behaviourism theory.

- Which strategies support a behaviourist approach and which move away from this?

- Does the policy lean more heavily to a positive reinforcement, negative reinforcement or punishment-based approach?

- Are there allowances for autonomy to ignore or adapt rules to be inclusive?

FURTHER READING

ITTECF 1.5. A culture of mutual trust and respect supports effective relationships.

A study by PISA (2015), entitled *Do Teacher–Student Relations Affect Students' Well-Being at School?*, asked students to evaluate their happiness at school across a range of OECD countries. From this 80 per cent of the students agreed or strongly agreed with the statement 'I feel happy at school.' PISA suggested that this was due to a positive and constructive teacher–student relationship, from which schools can foster the social and emotional well-being of students. This coincided and correlated with the study's finding on students' performance in maths, where students who reported they had good relationships with their teachers performed better. Students in these incidences felt they were listened to, treated fairly and received extra help when needed. It was noted they were less likely to report feeling lonely or like an outsider when these relationships were positive. There were also reports of fewer students arriving late for school or skipping classes or days of school where better teacher–student relationships were present. Schools felt the social and emotional development of their students were just as important as a students' mastery of subject skills and knowledge. Therefore, PISA concluded that good teacher–student relationships play an important part in the development of students' attitudes towards learning and as a result of this both their performance and sense of belonging at school benefit.

REFERENCES

Coughlan, S. (2021). The Big Interview: Doug Lemov. *Schools Week*, 23 October. https://schoolsweek.co.uk/the-big-interview-doug-lemov/. Accessed 19 November 2025.

Department for Education (DfE) (2019). *Initial Teacher Training (ITT): Core Content Framework*. Available at: www.gov.uk/government/publications/initial-teacher-training-itt-core-content-framework. Accessed 19 November 2025.

Dozier, C. L., Foley, E. A., Goddard, K. S. and Jess, R. L. (2019). Reinforcement. *The Encyclopedia of Child and Adolescent Development*, December, 1–10.

Dad, H., Ali, R., Janjua, M. Z. Q., Shahzad, S. and Khan, M. S. (2010). Comparison of the frequency and effectiveness of positive and negative reinforcement practices in schools. *Contemporary Issues in Education Research*, 3(1), 127–36.

Lemov, D. (2015). *Teach Like a Champion 2.0*. Hoboken, NJ: John Wiley & Sons.

Pavlov, I. P. (1927). *Conditioned Reflexes: An Investigation of the Physiological Activity of the Cerebral Cortex*. Oxford: Oxford University Press.

PISA (2015). *PISA in Focus: Do Teacher–Student Relations Affect Students' Well-Being at School?* Available at: www.oecd.org/en/publications/2015/04/do-teacher-student-relations-affect-students-well-being-at-school_g17a2623.html. Accessed 19 November 2025.

Skinner, B. F. (1957). *Verbal Behavior*. Acton, MA: Copley.

Staufenberg, J. (2021). The big interview with Doug Lemov. *Schools Week*. Available at: https://schoolsweek.co.uk/the-big-interview-doug-lemov/. Accessed 17 September 2024.

Thorndike, E. (1898). Animal intelligence: an experimental study of the associative processes in animals. Doctoral dissertation, Columbia University.

Timbrell, A. (2024). The power of positive reinforcement for children. *Educater*. Available at: www.educater.co.uk/latest-news/the-power-of-positive-reinforcement-for-children/. Accessed 17 September 2024.

Watson, J. B. (1913). Psychology as the behaviorist views it. *Psychological Review, 20*, 158–78.

Watson, J. B. (1930). *Behaviorism*, rev. edn. Chicago: University of Chicago Press.

5
COGNITIVISM

LEARNING OUTCOMES

By reading this chapter you will develop:

- An understanding of the role of memory (working memory, long-term memory, cognitive load) in pupil learning and classroom practice
- An understanding of how to apply cognitivist strategies such as retrieval practice, spaced learning, interleaving and dual coding
- An understanding of the concept of schema and how prior knowledge influences new learning
- An understanding of how to use metacognitive techniques to support pupils in becoming reflective and independent learners

INITIAL TEACHER TRAINING AND EARLY CAREER FRAMEWORK (ITTECF)

The key reading from the ITTECF that we must explore within this chapter is:

Sweller, J. (1988). Cognitive load during problem solving: effects on learning. *Cognitive Science*, *12*(2), 257-85. https://doi.org/10.1207/s15516709cog1202_4

INTRODUCTION

Cognitive science is not a new field, but specific key elements of cognitive science have evolved to become hugely influential within educational policy for England. It is central to the Initial Teacher Training and Early Career Framework (ITTECF) and all national professional qualifications (NPQs) which are taken by teachers and leaders. This evolution has taken place over the last 15 years and it is important to appreciate just how and why this has occurred. The main area of cognitive science that has influenced policy and practice in England is the notion of cognitive load theory (CLT).

PRINCIPLES OF COGNITIVISM

Cognitivism views learning as an internal process of acquiring, organising and storing information. It focuses on how learners process information, develop mental representations (schemas) and retrieve knowledge from memory.

Core principles:

- *information processing*: the mind is likened to a computer that receives, processes and stores information. Learning involves encoding information into long-term memory;

- *working memory and cognitive load*: learning is affected by the limitations of working memory. Instruction should be designed to avoid overload;

- *retrieval practice*: recalling information strengthens memory and improves long-term retention;

- *scaffolding*: support is provided to help learners process new information, gradually removed as competence increases;

- *schema theory*: learners build mental frameworks (schemas) that help them organise and interpret new information;

- *metacognition*: learners benefit from reflecting on their own thinking and learning strategies.

MEMORY (WORKING MEMORY, LONG-TERM MEMORY, COGNITIVE LOAD)

Kirschner et al. (2006) suggest that before information can be stored in long-term memory and organised into knowledge structures (schemas), it must first pass through a temporary mental workspace known as working memory. This part of the brain has a limited capacity, often cited as being able to hold between five and nine pieces of information at once (Miller, 1956), although this capacity can vary between individuals. The mental effort required to process information in working memory is referred to as *cognitive load*. When too much information is presented at once, the system becomes overloaded and the process of transferring knowledge into long-term memory (*encoding*) is disrupted (Kirschner et al., 2006). In practical terms, this means pupils may struggle to retain or understand new concepts.

Willingham (2009: 61) tells us that 'Memory is the residue of thought.' Pupils will remember what they think about and are more likely to learn what they actively pay attention to. CLT helps teachers understand why it is important to minimise distractions and ensure pupils' attention is directed towards the key learning points. Willingham (2009) notes that teachers sometimes unintentionally contribute to cognitive overload by including unnecessary or irrelevant details in lessons. While we may be vigilant about managing classroom behaviour, which can cause obvious distractions, we should also reflect on whether our teaching content is focused and purposeful. Willingham suggests that, to teach well, teachers should pay attention to what the task will actually make pupils think about because that is what they will remember (2009).

THE RISE OF COGNITIVE LOAD THEORY

The main area of cognitive science that has influenced policy and practice in England is the notion of cognitive load theory (CLT), a framework in psychology explaining how working memory processes information. It has become a dominant force in England's schools and the ITTECF, as well as being essential for every NPQ taken by teachers, senior leaders, SENDCos and others to help learn how to run schools. Developed by Sweller in the late 1980s, CLT's influence has grown steadily over the decades (Sweller, 1988). Sweller's initial research focused on problem-solving, where he observed that learners frequently employed a strategy known as *means-ends analysis* (a way of solving problems by breaking them down into smaller steps). While seemingly intuitive, this approach can inadvertently overload working memory, hindering rather than helping the learning process (Sweller, 1988).

During the 1990s, CLT gained traction within educational research. Studies demonstrated the effectiveness of applying CLT principles to instructional design (Mayer and Moreno, 2003). Researchers discovered that by deliberately reducing cognitive load, learners were better equipped to process information and improve retention (Sweller, 1994). This recognition of the limitations of working memory and the importance of managing its load marked a significant shift in pedagogical thinking.

The early 2000s saw CLT principles translated into practical instructional techniques. Approaches such as worked *examples, the split-attention effect and the modality effect* emerged as methods for minimising extraneous cognitive load and optimising learning (Mayer, 2005). Worked examples provide learners with step-by-step solutions, reducing the need for them to generate solutions from scratch. The split-attention effect addresses the problem of information being presented in a way that requires learners to mentally integrate disparate sources. A typical example would be a teacher presenting a labelled diagram while talking about the model being presented. A student will be trying to make sense of the diagram and listen to the teacher simultaneously and end up either ignoring the teacher or the diagram. The modality effect leverages the strengths of different sensory modalities (e.g., combining visual and auditory information) to reduce load on a single channel. You may have heard of the idea of using dual coding during teaching, an approach that draws on these principles – for example, a teacher might explain a historical event while simultaneously showing relevant images or a timeline. This dual presentation helps learners create stronger mental representations and improve recall. It is important to note that simply adding images is not the aim – it is about delivering information efficiently across the two channels.

By the 2010s, CLT had become increasingly influential in teacher training and professional development programmes in England. School leaders began to receive CPD which presented the idea of understanding cognitive limitations and designing lessons that aligned with CLT principles (Perry et al., 2021); they then organised in-school CPD to help disseminate these principles and how they should be used in teaching.

Sweller (1988) identifies three types of cognitive load:

- *intrinsic load* relates to the complexity of the material itself, which can vary depending on pupils' prior knowledge and the abstract nature of the content;

- *extraneous load* refers to how the material is presented – this could include unclear instructions or language that is difficult to understand;

- *germane load* involves the mental effort required to build and strengthen long-term memory.

Sweller also acknowledges that learners differ in their ability to process information, influenced by factors such as age, prior knowledge, skill level and socio-economic background. Understanding these differences can help teachers tailor their instruction to better support all pupils, and will help them to connect personally with pupils, which as Willingham reminds us, is one of the key properties of being a good teacher (2009).

COGNITIVIST STRATEGIES FOR LEARNING (RETRIEVAL PRACTICE, SPACED LEARNING, INTERLEAVING)

Three main strategies from cognitivist psychology that have been recognised to be particularly effective at supporting pupil learning by strengthening memories and enhancing long-term retention are *retrieval practice, spaced learning* and *interleaving* (Dunlosky et al., 2013).

RETRIEVAL PRACTICE

To be effective, retrieval practice requires some effort from pupils to actively bring knowledge to mind from memory (Weinstein et al., 2018); it will not be achieved by reviewing notes or by the teacher re-teaching materials (Bates and Shea, 2024). Retrieval can take many forms, such as self-testing or taking practice tests, using flashcards, writing what you remember, or teaching someone else. Additionally, to be effective retrieval should be low-pressure, such as through informal quizzes or short recall tasks in the classroom; high-stakes testing can increase anxiety and hinder memory formation. However, McMahon et al. (2021) remind us that some pupils may find low-stakes retrieval challenging and may need encouragement to persist through the discomfort until they are familiar with the process.

SPACED LEARNING

Spaced learning, also known as distributed practice, involves revisiting content after a period of time rather than cramming it all into one session. Research shows that spreading out study time improves retention compared to *massed practice* (cramming). Bjork and Bjork (2011) offer an explanation for why spaced learning is so effective, grounded in their distinction between two key components of memory:

- *storage strength*, which reflects how well learned or entrenched a memory is;
- *retrieval strength*, which reflects how accessible a memory is at a given moment.

Retrieval strength can fluctuate based on recent use and contextual cues, so spaced learning works because when information is not used, such as when a topic has been studied some months ago, its retrieval strength declines and the learner is forced to work harder to retrieve the information. This effortful retrieval boosts storage strength (Weinstein et al., 2018), which makes the memory more robust and resistant to forgetting. In contrast, massed practice (cramming) keeps retrieval strength artificially high, leading to easier recall in the short term but weaker long-term retention (Willingham, 2009). However, McMahon et al. (2021) caution us that the ideal spacing interval isn't clearly defined and may vary depending on the content and the learners; teachers' professional judgement as to when to instigate spaced learning remains essential.

INTERLEAVING

Interleaving involves mixing different but related types of content within a single learning session (e.g., ABC, ABC, ABC). For example, in maths, pupils might alternate between calculating the area of rectangles and triangles (McMahon et al., 2021). This contrasts with blocking, which is when you practice one topic or skill repeatedly before moving on to the next (e.g., AAA, BBB, CCC). Pan (2015) highlights the benefits of interleaving as a learning strategy, arguing that it forces the brain to work harder to retrieve the right strategy or concept, which strengthens learning, suggesting that it helps learners spot differences and similarities between concepts, improving understanding and flexibility. Additionally, interleaving prepares learners for real-world situations, where problems are rarely presented in neat, predictable blocks. However, as McMahon et al. (2021) remind us, it's important to strike a balance; too much switching can be counterproductive. As with spaced learning, applying interleaving effectively requires thoughtful planning and professional judgement.

DUAL CODING THEORY

Dual coding is a teaching and learning strategy grounded in cognitive psychology, particularly the work of Allan Paivio. It's especially useful for teachers because it helps pupils process and retain information more effectively by engaging both verbal and visual systems in the brain. According to Paivio's *dual coding theory* (1971), our brains process information through two channels:

- a *verbal channel* (for words, spoken or written);
- a *visual channel* (for images, diagrams, spatial layouts).

Sweller's cognitive load theory suggests that effective working memory capacity can be increased by using both visual and auditory working memory rather than either processor alone. Dual coding is seen as beneficial because it:

- distributes cognitive load across two channels – visual and auditory;

- supports schema construction by helping learners integrate new information with prior knowledge;

- improves encoding and recall by presenting information in multiple formats that reinforce each other.

Sweller hypothesised that two channels are better than one and combining words and images effectively facilitates learning; if the same information is offered properly in two different ways, it enables one to access more working memory capacity. It also allows one to remember or recognise the information in two different ways. When both channels are activated and the information is meaningfully connected, it creates stronger memory traces. This helps pupils:

- understand complex ideas more easily;

- recall information more accurately;

- transfer knowledge to new contexts.

Mayer's (2019) empirical research demonstrated that learners who received explanations with both text and relevant visuals consistently performed better on understanding and transfer tasks than those who received only text or only visuals.

SCHEMA THEORY

Schema theory is a foundational idea in cognitive psychology that helps explain how we organise, store and retrieve knowledge. Essentially, a schema is a mental framework of background knowledge, like a map or blueprint, that helps us interpret the world. For example, when someone says 'classroom' to you, your schema will be recalled which might include desks, a teacher, a whiteboard and pupils. When you enter a new classroom, you draw on this schema to quickly understand what's going on. Piaget proposed that when new information fits into an existing schema, it is assimilated. When it doesn't fit, the schema must be accommodated – that is, adjusted to incorporate the new learning (Piaget, 1952). For example, as you experience different settings your schema for 'classroom' might expand to include the aspects of different subjects' classrooms, such as the science lab or the art room, and different types of classroom layouts. This accommodation process is essential for conceptual change, but it can also reveal misconceptions. As pupils discuss their prior understanding of a topic they may reveal faulty schemas (misconceptions) that need to be reshaped through careful teaching and scaffolding.

The role of prior knowledge in learning has long been recognised in educational theory (Ausubel, 1968) and we know that learning is most effective when new information interacts meaningfully with what's already stored in long-term memory. If new content does not connect with what pupils already know, it's unlikely to be retained (Howard-Jones et al., 2020). This prior knowledge isn't limited to facts, it also includes emotions, beliefs, physical experiences and skills, and can take many forms:

- *declarative*: facts, such as knowing the name of the prime minister;

- *sensory*: such as knowing what freshly baked bread smells and tastes like;

- *narrative*: such as understanding story structures from books or TV;

- *embodied*: developed through lived experience, such as balance or rhythm.

These past experiences influence how pupils interpret and retain new information (McMahon et al., 2021). Teachers therefore need to help pupils access relevant schema. For example, when teaching topics such as war poetry in English, pupils may have relevant schema from history lessons to draw upon, along with schema from previous experiences of poetry lessons. Additionally, they may have heard loud noises in the past or felt the emotions of fear in different contexts. All these experiences can be drawn upon to help pupils to create a new schema for war poetry which they can add to as they move forward with the topic.

It is important for teachers to remember that emotional states play a critical role in cognitive functioning, particularly in relation to attention, working memory and memory retrieval (Howard-Jones, 2018). Negative emotions such as stress or anxiety can impair a learner's ability to process and recall information, even when that information has been well encoded. Conversely, positive emotional states can enhance cognitive performance by increasing engagement and supporting neurochemical processes that aid memory consolidation. Importantly, Howard-Jones argues that emotion and cognition are not separate systems but operate in an integrated manner within the brain, suggesting that emotionally supportive learning environments are essential for effective teaching and learning.

METACOGNITIVIST TECHNIQUES

Metacognition is best understood as a key component of *self-regulated learning* (SRL), which also includes emotional and motivational aspects of learning. It involves pupils taking ownership of their learning and actively engaging in the process. According to Muijs and Bokhove (2020), SRL consists of three interconnected elements:

- *cognition*: refers to the mental strategies used during learning, such as focusing attention, rehearsing information and elaborating on ideas;

- *metacognition*: involves the ability to plan, monitor and evaluate one's own learning. It includes knowing how you learn best and choosing appropriate strategies to support that;

- *motivation*: encompasses beliefs about one's ability to succeed (self-efficacy), interest in the task and emotional responses. Because regulating thinking takes effort, motivation plays a vital role – learners need to be able to delay gratification and understand that short-term effort leads to long-term gains.

Experienced teachers will recognise that much of their work involves creating a classroom environment that supports SRL. This might include setting clear expectations, modelling what success looks like, using peer and self-assessment and encouraging reflection during plenaries. Teachers also help pupils learn how to concentrate and how to learn from mistakes. While some pupils may pick up these habits naturally, it's important for teachers to make these strategies explicit by explaining how and why they support learning, and by narrating their own worked examples as they provide models, so that pupils can see how metacognitive strategies are used 'live'. It's also worth remembering that we're not always the best judges of our own performance; we tend to view our work more positively than others might (Burnett, 2016). This is why clear criteria and constructive feedback are essential.

The Education Endowment Foundation (EEF) report by Muijs and Bokhove (2020: pp. 25–6) outlines three categories of strategies within SRL:

- *cognitive strategies*: activities like rehearsal, reviewing, retrieval practice and spaced learning;

- *metacognitive strategies*: planning, selecting strategies, monitoring progress and adjusting approaches based on reflection;

- *social-emotional strategies*: managing motivation and relationships, including delaying gratification, building self-efficacy and seeking help when needed.

It's important to note that measuring metacognition is challenging – there's no single method that works for all learners (Muijs and Bokhove, 2020). Some researchers argue that metacognition depends on subject-specific knowledge, meaning it shouldn't be treated as a standalone skill. However, the EEF review suggests that improving SRL and metacognitive skills can lead to better academic outcomes.

Since SRL relies on drawing from prior knowledge, it's essential to recognise the diversity of pupils' experiences and backgrounds. While it's important to avoid stereotyping, research shows that social background can influence the development of metacognitive skills, though the relationship is modest (Muijs and Bokhove, 2020).

CRITICISMS OF COGNITIVISM

Drawing on the ITTECF, this chapter examined how cognitive principles are embedded in teacher development, particularly in areas such as retrieval practice, dual coding, sequencing and metacognition. These strategies help pupils manage cognitive load, build connections between ideas and reflect on their own learning processes.

However, it has to be noted that the integration of learning sciences into the education of teachers is not without challenges. The *Core Content Framework* (DfE, 2019) (which has now been supplanted by the ITTECF) mandated by the DfE in England, for example, has been criticised for its narrow focus on learning theories. In addition to excluding traditional foundational knowledge about behaviourism, constructivism and social constructivism, it omits research from neuroscience and education, as well as studies on neurodiversity and executive function, which are crucial for understanding diverse learning needs (Shea, 2024). This exclusion is seen as ideological rather than academic (Hordern and Brooks, 2023) and that is an issue for higher education institutions (HEIs) and providers of teacher education (not all providers are HEIs) who are further regulated by the Quality Assurance Agency for Higher Education (QAA) and are required to offer their teacher trainees the full breadth of research and theoretical understanding necessary for effective teaching.

HEIs in England often address these gaps by incorporating a broader range of research into their teacher education programmes, as expected by the QAA. However, not all institutions follow this approach. Some align closely with the DfE's ideological stance, influenced by financial dependencies or political motivations. There are substantial teacher education providers in England who have promoted an exclusive approach to cognitivism as part of their delivery of teacher education and who have influenced the emergence of, first, the CCF and then the ITTECF, with their narrow and politicised approaches to how learning sciences should be used in teaching. Such institutions vary from Teach First, established in 2002, to the EEF, established in 2011, right up to the more recent National Institute for Teacher Education (NIFTE), established in 2024 just before the end of the 2010–24 Conservative-led UK government administrations.

CONSIDER THIS: THE DIVERSITY OF LEARNERS

Consider the idea that we need to think about the diversity of learners when applying cognitivism to our teaching. In reflecting on this, ask yourself the following questions.

- How do I ensure that cognitive strategies are inclusive and accessible for learners with a range of backgrounds, abilities and learning needs?

- What methods do I use to reflect on and evaluate the impact of cognitive strategies in my classroom, and how do these reflections inform my future planning?

PRACTICAL APPLICATION

Many schools and trusts implement a policy requiring teachers to begin each lesson with a short, focused do now task. These tasks often involve:

- retrieval practice of previously taught content;

- low-stakes quizzing to reinforce memory;

- activating prior knowledge relevant to the upcoming lesson.

This policy is grounded in cognitivist principles, particularly the importance of retrieval practice, schema activation and reducing cognitive load by linking new learning to existing knowledge. It also supports consistent routines that enhance memory and engagement across subjects.

You will be encouraged to carry out observations of expert others across the curriculum; one focus for these observations might be looking at how cognitivist strategies are employed across the curriculum. See Table 5.1 on the next page for a helpful guide to what to look out for.

CASE STUDY: USING COGNITIVIST APPROACHES IN A KEY STAGE 3 POETRY LESSON

Context: Imagine a Key Stage 3 English teacher at a mixed comprehensive school is teaching a Year 8 class a lesson on the poem 'Half-caste' by John Agard. Her aim is to help pupils understand the poem's themes, structure and use of language, while also encouraging deeper engagement with its cultural context.

Table 5.1 *Cognitivist strategies across subjects*

Cognitivist strategy	Science (photosynthesis)	History (English Civil War)	English (poetry analysis)
Activating prior knowledge	Concept map on plant needs to link new content to existing schema	Quiz on Tudor monarchy and Reformation to activate relevant schema	Brainstorming prior experiences with poetry and literary devices
Dual coding	Diagram of photosynthesis with verbal explanation and colour coding	Images and short texts (e.g., Charles I, parliament) annotated by pupils	Annotated poem with visual symbols for metaphor, tone and structure
Chunking and sequencing	Step-by-step breakdown of photosynthesis process	Separate introduction of political, religious and economic causes	Breaking poem into stanzas and analysing one device at a time
Retrieval practice	Mini whiteboard quiz on key terms and processes	Quiz on prior learning and key causes of conflict	Quick-fire questions on poetic techniques and terminology
Scaffolding	Paired diagram completion with teacher prompts	Guided comparison worksheet with evaluative questions	Sentence starters for analysing poetic meaning and effect
Advance organisers	Concept map and lesson overview	Timeline and thematic concept map (monarchy, parliament, religion)	Graphic organiser showing poetic devices and their effects
Metacognitive reflection	Exit questions on learning strategies and understanding	Paragraph reflection on most important cause and reasoning	Reflection on how interpretation changed during analysis
Cognitive load management	Structured note templates and simplified explanations	Clear sequencing and focused content delivery	Focused analysis tasks with reduced distractions and clear objectives

COGNITIVIST STRATEGIES APPLIED

1. *Activating prior knowledge (schema theory)*

   The teacher begins the lesson with a short discussion on identity and language, asking pupils to reflect on words they've encountered that relate to mixed heritage. This primes pupils' existing schemas and prepares them to connect new ideas to familiar concepts.

2. *Dual coding*

   The teacher presents the poem alongside a visual representation – a mind map showing key themes such as race, identity and language. Pupils annotate the poem with symbols and colours that correspond to these themes, reinforcing understanding through both verbal and visual channels.

3. *Chunking and sequencing*

   The poem is broken into manageable sections. Each stanza is explored individually, focusing on one literary device at a time (e.g., metaphor, repetition, tone). This helps pupils process information without overwhelming their working memory.

4. *Retrieval practice*

   Midway through the lesson, pupils complete a short quiz on poetic devices previously studied in the unit. This reinforces prior learning and strengthens long-term memory, allowing pupils to apply these concepts to the current poem.

5. *Scaffolding*

   Pupils are given sentence starters to support their analysis, such as 'The poet uses repetition to ...' and 'This metaphor suggests ...'. These scaffolds are gradually removed as pupils gain confidence in expressing their interpretations.

6. *Metacognitive reflection*

   At the end of the lesson, pupils write a brief reflection: 'What helped you understand the poem today?' and 'What strategy will you use to analyse a poem next time?' This encourages them to think about their own learning processes and develop metacognitive awareness.

OUTCOMES

Pupils demonstrate a deeper understanding of the poem's meaning and structure. They are able to articulate how Agard uses language to challenge stereotypes and express identity. The use of cognitivist strategies supports both comprehension and engagement, particularly for pupils who benefit from structured, scaffolded learning.

CHAPTER SUMMARY

While behaviourism focuses on external behaviours and constructivism emphasises social and experiential learning, cognitivism bridges the gap by focusing on the mental processes that underpin learning. It provides a scientific foundation for many classroom strategies now embedded in the DfE's Initial Teacher Training and Early Career Framework, such as retrieval practice, dual coding and sequencing.

This chapter has provided an overview of cognitivism and cognitive load theory, a learning theory developed from cognitive science. Among the major theories of learning, cognitivism offers a compelling framework that focuses on the internal mental processes involved in acquiring and organising knowledge. It is a learning theory that explains how information is received, processed, stored and retrieved by the mind. Cognitivism provides an approach to learning that encourages learners to use their brain more effectively by thinking about their own learning processes and *learning how to learn*. Unlike behaviourism, which emphasises observable behaviours and external stimuli, cognitivism views learners as active processors of information, capable of constructing meaning through attention, memory and reasoning. Pupils are encouraged to bring their own experiences to the learning which can increase engagement and motivation as they begin to feel a connection with the learning process. Cognitivist theory posits that learning occurs when learners actively engage with content, organise it into existing mental frameworks (schemas) and apply it in meaningful ways. Learning involves active mental engagement, where learners process information, form connections with prior knowledge and develop internal representations or schemas. These processes are influenced by factors such as attention, memory and metacognition.

REFLECTIVE QUESTIONS: CHAPTER 5

Reflecting on the idea that most approaches to teaching and learning blend ideas from multiple learning sciences, reflect on the idea of cognitivism. Think about the following in reflecting on this.

- How do I currently integrate strategies from cognitivism – such as retrieval practice, dual coding, or sequencing – alongside techniques drawn from behaviourist or constructivist approaches?

- Can I think of a specific lesson or unit where applying cognitive principles helped pupils make meaningful links between ideas or concepts?

- How do whole-school routines – like do now tasks or the use of knowledge organisers – reflect principles of memory, schema development and cognitive load management?

FURTHER READING

ITTECF 2.2 Prior knowledge plays an important role in how pupils learn; committing some key facts to their long-term memory is likely to help pupils learn more complex ideas.

Willingham, D. (2009). *Why Don't Students Like School? A Cognitive Scientist Answers Questions About How the Mind Works and What it Means for the Classroom*. San Francisco: Jossey-Bass.

In this book, Willingham argues that many difficulties students face in school stem from misunderstandings about how learning works. He emphasises that cognitive science can offer practical guidance for improving teaching and learning and offers suggestions for teachers that can be useful for their classroom work.

REFERENCES

Ausubel, D. P. (1968). *Educational Psychology: A Cognitive View*. Austin, TX: Holt, Rinehart & Winston.

Bates, G. and Shea, J. (2024). Retrieval practice in the wild. *Mind, Brain and Education, 18*(3), 249–57.

Bjork, E. L. and Bjork, R. A. (2011). Making things hard on yourself, but in a good way: creating desirable difficulties to enhance learning. In M. A. Gernsbacher, R. W. Pew, L. M. Hough and J. R. Pomerantz (eds), *Psychology and the Real World: Essays Illustrating Fundamental Contributions to Society*. Bury St Edmunds: Worth, pp. 56–64.

Burnett, D. (2016). *The Idiot Brain: A Neuroscientist Explains What Your Head is Really Up To*. London: Guardian Faber.

Department for Education (DfE) (2014). *School Admissions Code*. London: DfE.

DfE (2019). *Initial Teacher Training (ITT): Core Content Framework*. Available at: www.gov.uk/government/publications/initial-teacher-training-itt-core-content-framework. Accessed 19 November 2025.

DfE (2024). *Initial Teacher Training and Early Career Framework*. Available at: www.gov.uk/government/publications/initial-teacher-training-and-early-career-framework. Accessed 19 November 2025.

DfE (2025). *Special Educational Needs in England*. Available at: https://explore-education-statistics.service.gov.uk/find-statistics/special-educational-needs-in-england. Accessed 19 November 2025.

Dunlosky, J., Rawson, K. A., Marsh, E. J., Nathan, M. J. and Willingham, D. T. (2013). Improving students' learning with effective learning techniques: promising directions from cognitive and educational psychology. *Psychological Science in the Public Interest, 14*(1), 4–58.

Hordern, J. and Brooks, C. (2023). The Core Content Framework and the 'new science' of educational research. *Oxford Review of Education, 49*(1), 1–19.

Howard-Jones, P. (2018). *Evolution of the Learning Brain: Or How You Got to be So Smart …* London: Routledge.

Howard-Jones, P., Ioannou, K., Bailey, R., Prior, J., Jay, T. and Yau, S. (2020). Towards a science of teaching and learning for teacher education. In M. S. C. Thomas, D. Mareschal and I. Dumontheil (eds), *Educational Neuroscience: Development Across the Lifespan*. London: Routledge, pp. 445–73.

Kirschner, P. A., Sweller, J. and Clark, R. E. (2006). Why minimal guidance during instruction does not work: an analysis of the failure of constructivist, discovery, problem-based, experiential, and inquiry-based teaching. *Educational Psychologist, 41*(2), 75–86.

Mayer, R. E. (2005). *Cambridge Handbook of Multimedia Learning*. Cambridge: Cambridge University Press.

Mayer, R. E. (2019). How multimedia can improve learning and instruction. In J. Dunlosky and K. A. Rawson (eds), *The Cambridge Handbook of Cognition and Education*. Cambridge: Cambridge University Press, pp. 460–79.

Mayer, R. E. and Moreno, R. (2003). Nine ways to reduce cognitive load in multimedia learning. *Educational Psychologist, 38*(1), 43–52.

McMahon, K., Lee, A., Etchells, P. J., Howarth, L., Humphreys, K., McKay, D., Arblaster, E., Asprey, E., Barber, K.-A. and Salter, L. (2021). *The Learning Sciences and the Core Content Framework for Initial Teacher Training*. Bath: Bath Spa University.

Miller, G. A. (1956). Information and memory. *Scientific American, 195*(2), 42–7.

Muijs, D. and Bokhove, C. (2020). *Metacognition and Self-Regulation: Evidence Review*. London: EEF.

Pan, C. (2015). The interleaving effect: mixing it up boosts learning. *Scientific American*, August.

Paivio, A. (1971). *Imagery and verbal processes*. Austin, TX: Holt, Rinehart & Winston.

Perry, T., Lea, R., Jørgensen, C. R., Cordingley, P., Shapiro, K. and Youdell, D. (2021). *Cognitive Science in the Classroom*. London: EEF. Available at: https://potentialplusuk.org/wp-content/uploads/2022/02/Cognitive_Science_in_the_classroom_-_Evidence_and_practice_.pdf. Accessed 3 December 2025.

Piaget, J. (1952). *The Origins of Intelligence in Children*. Madison, CT: International Universities Press.

Shea, J. (2024). The hidden voice of pre-service teachers in their private social media interactions. In J. Wearmouth and A. Goodwyn (eds), *Pupil, Teacher and Student Voice in Educational Institutions: Values, Opinions, Beliefs and Perspectives*. London: Routledge.

Sweller, J. (1988). Cognitive load during problem solving: effects on learning. *Cognitive Science*, *12*(2), 257–85.

Sweller, J. (1994). Cognitive load theory, learning difficulty, and instructional design. *Learning and Instruction*, *4*(4), 295–312.

Weinstein, Y., Sumeraki, M. and Caviglioli, O. (2018). *Understanding How We Learn: A Visual Guide*. London: Routledge.

Willingham, D. (2009). *Why Don't Students Like School? A Cognitive Scientist Answers Questions About How the Mind Works and What it Means for the Classroom*. San Francisco: Jossey-Bass.

6

CONSTRUCTIVISM

LEARNING OUTCOMES

By reading this chapter you will develop:

- An understanding of the core research and theories underpinning constructivism
- An understanding of some of the approaches to incorporating constructivist strategies into teaching practice
- An understanding of some of the risks and limitations of the constructivist approach

INITIAL TEACHER TRAINING AND EARLY CAREER FRAMEWORK (ITTECF)

The key reading from the ITTECF that is to be explored within this chapter is:

Van de Pol, J., Volman, M., Oort, F. and Beishuizen, J. (2015). The effects of scaffolding in the classroom: support contingency and student independent working time in relation to student achievement, task effort and appreciation of support. *Instructional Science*, 43(5), 615–41.

INTRODUCTION

Constructivism is a theory that emphasises the active role of learners in building their own understanding of the world, rather than passively receiving information (Piaget, 1972). This chapter will explore the core research and principles underpinning constructivism, drawing on the work of key theorists such as Piaget, Vygotsky and Bruner, and will discuss how knowledge is constructed through experiences and interactions with the environment and others. Furthermore, this chapter will examine practical constructivist strategies for teaching and learning, alongside considering their potential risks and limitations.

MAJOR THEORISTS

According to Piaget (1972), children do not passively absorb information but rather actively make sense of it, continuously adapting their mental models through a process of assimilation and accommodation. Piaget believed that learners actively construct their own knowledge by interacting with their environment and progressing through stages of cognitive development. He highlighted the importance of hands-on learning and problem-solving in developing cognitive growth.

Vygotsky (1978), another major figure in constructivism, added to the theory with his concept of the zone of proximal development (ZPD), which refers to the space between what a learner can do independently and what they can do with assistance. Vygotsky's work highlights the importance of social interaction in cognitive development, suggesting that learning is inherently social and that through guided interaction with more knowledgeable peers or teachers learners can build on their understanding and move beyond what they can achieve alone.

Bruner (1960) contributed to the theory by encouraging learning by discovery, where learners actively explore and discover concepts for themselves rather than being taught in a traditional, didactic manner. Bruner suggested that learners should be encouraged to engage in problem-solving tasks that require them to apply concepts in real-world contexts, thereby developing deeper understanding. He also stressed the importance of scaffolding, where teachers provide temporary support to help learners achieve tasks they cannot complete independently, but can master with guidance.

KEY PRINCIPLES OF CONSTRUCTIVISM

A key principle of constructivism is that learning is deeply personal and contextual. As learners interact with their environment, they bring their prior knowledge, experiences and cultural background into the learning process. This makes learning highly individual and underlines the importance of creating an educational environment that is responsive to the learner's needs (Bruner, 1960). Additionally, constructivism advocates for an assessment approach that focuses on the learner's understanding and ability to apply knowledge rather than rote memorisation.

Consequently, in education, constructivist approaches often promote enquiry-based learning, collaborative learning and active problem-solving. These methods support the idea that learning should be a process of exploring and understanding, where students are encouraged to ask questions, challenge assumptions and engage in critical thinking. Therefore, the key aspects of constructivist classrooms include:

- *active learning*: where students are involved in the learning process through exploration, problem-solving and enquiry;

- *collaborative learning*: the idea that learning is a social activity, with students working together to share knowledge and solve problems;

- *scaffolding*: where teachers provide temporary support to help learners reach tasks they cannot accomplish alone (Vygotsky, 1978);

- *contextual learning*: where lessons are rooted in real-world contexts to make learning meaningful (Bruner, 1960).

THE FURTHER DEVELOPMENT OF CONSTRUCTIVISM

Kagan (1994) took this basic principle and developed a series of structures and techniques based on collaborative learning designed to foster student interaction, engagement and teamwork. These structures match closely to the principles of constructivism, which emphasise active learning, social interaction and student-driven knowledge construction. These structures, such as *think–pair–share*, *jigsaw* and *round robin*, promote peer interaction and allow students to engage in active learning, a core tenet of constructivism (Kagan, 1994).

For example, in think–pair–share, students are posed a question and given time to independently think about it before opening a discussion with their paired student to share their thoughts; finally, they share their ideas with the whole class. This encourages independent thinking as well as peer discussion and active participation.

In a jigsaw activity students are assigned different sections of a text and then collaborate with peers to share their findings, building a collective understanding of that text. In the round robin technique each participant contributes to a discussion in turn, sharing or responding to ideas, ensuring that everyone is involved in the discussion – again fostering collaborative learning as well as communication skills. Additionally, these structures provide scaffolding, as students help each other to construct knowledge, reinforcing the principles of the ZPD (Vygotsky, 1978).

In Kagan's cooperative structures, students work in pairs or small groups, where more capable peers can support less confident learners, supporting the development of deeper understanding. The use of Kagan structures also encourages student autonomy in learning. By engaging in collaborative activities, students take ownership of their learning, exploring concepts through discussion and problem-solving. Kagan's structures allow students to voice their thoughts, make decisions and test their ideas in a supportive environment, which is suggested by Bruner (1960) in his work on discovery learning.

CRITICISMS OF CONSTRUCTIVISM

Despite its many advantages, including its focus on active, student-centred learning, constructivism has also faced substantive criticisms, particularly around its practical implementation in a more diverse classroom setting. Critics argue that constructivist methods can be time-consuming, require extensive resources and may not always be feasible in large, standardised classrooms (Kirschner et al., 2006). Furthermore, the theory assumes that all students have the foundational knowledge to engage in discovery learning, which may not be the case. Many cognitivists argue that learning through discovery is inefficient and ineffective. Often, they argue, critical explicit semantic knowledge is best learned through direct instruction and then reinforced through repeated retrieval. They reason that unless foundational knowledge is learned well and is retrieved effortlessly, then higher order tasks will have extraneous load in the form of poor or unsuccessful retrieval. As this book has said repeatedly, such criticisms are valid and teachers using discovery learning through collaborative approaches to learn foundational and specific knowledge that requires successful retrieval should consider pedagogical ideas from cognitivism, which has a strong evidence base for creating cued recall for specific foundational knowledge.

One of the further main criticisms of constructivism is its lack of structure. Critics argue that without sufficient guidance, students may struggle to learn effectively, especially those who are less self-motivated or lack foundational knowledge. The hallmark of a teacher who has not successfully blended learning sciences is when you see group work which is unsuccessful. Kirschner et al. (2006) argue that minimal guidance approaches, such as those suggested by constructivism, can be ineffective in certain contexts – for example, where foundational knowledge or skills are missing, or the success criteria of task set is not obvious or clear. They suggest that direct instruction, where teachers explicitly teach content, is more effective in helping students acquire foundational knowledge and skills. According to this view, constructivism can lead to cognitive overload, particularly for students who are unfamiliar with the content, as they are expected to construct knowledge without sufficient scaffolding (Sweller, 1988).

Constructivism also assumes that all students are capable of independent learning and critical thinking, but this is not always the case. Students vary in their ability to engage with open-ended tasks and abstract concepts. Lower-attaining students may struggle with the lack of guidance and requirement for self-direction, leading to frustration and disengagement. Without sufficient support, these students may not reach the desired learning outcomes. Therefore, it could be argued that the more structured, teacher-led approach may be more beneficial (PISA, 2009).

Another concern is the time- and resource-intensive nature of the approach. Implementing hands-on, enquiry-based activities and collaborative projects can be demanding on both teachers and students. Constructivism requires teachers to be highly skilled in creating and managing interactive learning environments, which may not always be suitable for larger classrooms or under tight curriculum constraints. Furthermore, these methods may require significant preparation, including setting up projects, arranging group work, and providing continuous feedback throughout. This can be overwhelming, especially for teachers with limited resources or experience (Hattie, 2009). The reality could be that you are working in a school with substantial behaviour issues. In such an environment, pedagogical approaches which rely on maturity and professional collaboration could contribute to a poor overall sense of behaviour around a school. In such a situation, reducing the amount of collaboration available to students and increasing the amount of teacher-led pedagogy can be part of a behaviourist approach to reforming behaviour in a school environment. However, once that has been achieved, a school or trust should then take steps to rebalance the pedagogies being deployed in the school, otherwise the students in that school will never learn to collaborate with their peers – a specific and measurable trait which is valued worldwide – as evidenced by the Programme for International Student Assessment (PISA) which assesses students in four main areas:

- collaborative problem-solving;

- reading literacy;

- mathematical literacy;

- scientific literacy.

Lastly, concern about the assessment of learning in a constructivist setting can be considered. More traditional assessment, which generally focuses on factual recall and individual performance, may not match up to the assessment required by constructivism, which focuses more on the process of learning than the final product. This mismatch can make it difficult to measure student progress or provide accountability (Black and Wiliam, 1998).

CONCLUSION

Constructivism suggests that you need to allow the learners to be active participants in their learning and to build on their prior knowledge in the context of their view of the world. It promotes a collaborative and enquiry-based learning environment, allows students to explore, ask questions and process learning, leading to critical thinking and, eventually, understanding. The teacher therefore acts as a facilitator to this, where necessary, guiding students to achieve learning outcomes.

PRACTICAL APPLICATION

Constructivism advocates the active involvement of students in constructing their own understanding, based on personal experiences, problem-solving and social interactions. It has been seen to encourage students to take ownership of their knowledge which can lead to deeper learning and understanding.

CONSIDER THIS: CONSTRUCTIVISM IN YOUR LESSONS

Consider how you currently teach and how much constructivism, including social constructivism, is contained within your lessons.

- How often do you use group work and how successful is it when you do?

- When you lead question and answer sessions, do you explicitly set out to push your students through the ZPD?

- How well do you track that students have suitable prior knowledge before adding to their schemata?

SELF-EVALUATION AND CRITIQUE

Subject like art, English literature, drama and physical education probably offer the most obvious application of constructivist principles. Encouraging students to work collaboratively, or experiment with materials, techniques and forms, allowing them to make connections between their personal experience and the work they create, all leads to construction of knowledge. Instead of focusing on the final product, the learning process is prioritised as students engage in self-evaluation and critique, which develop not only their technical skills, but also their ability to reflect critically on their work. This in turn fosters creativity and self-expression as forms of problem-solving (Kagan, 1994).

For example, in subjects like art and drama the use of a reflective journal – wherein, at the end of each lesson throughout the creative process, students write a short entry describing and reflecting on their artistic choices, the challenges they faced and what they learned – can help them self-evaluate their practice and consider how they might move forward next lesson. Pairing this with a before and after analysis of their original idea versus their final product can further help them identify what they have changed and improved, and the techniques used to do so. Using simple and clear checklists or marking rubrics during this would support students in being able to identify and understand the assessment criteria and provide them with a clear structure to work to, as well as helping them set specific goals or actions to carry out moving forwards. These could include 'improving shading' or 'making the composition more dynamic' in art and 'include a freeze frame' or 'use body language to develop the portrayal of a characters emotion' in drama. This process could also be carried out in a peer-review format where other students in the class use the assessment criteria checklist to provide constructive feedback. This is often beneficial as it not only provides a new perspective on the work, but also develops students' evaluation and communication skills.

CRITICAL THINKING AND PROBLEM-SOLVING

However, constructivist approaches can be utilised in a range of other subjects – for example, mathematics is a subject which is heavily founded in the use of critical thinking and problem-solving skills. This can be done through the constructivist lens by exploring mathematical concepts through real-world applications, such as budgeting, cooking measurements or travel time calculations. Also, when teaching geometry, for instance, the teacher may use manipulatives or interactive software which allows the student to physically explore shapes and their properties, allowing them to build connections between abstract concepts and concrete experiences (Bruner, 1960). Allowing students to formulate their own strategies and solutions to enquiry-based problem-solving tasks can help them develop mathematical reasoning and critical thinking (Hattie, 2009). Activities like maths escape rooms, where each solved maths problem 'unlocks' the next clue in a puzzle or escape room scenario, are a good way of developing this as they not only require reasoning and critical thinking skills to solve each puzzle, but also for working out which of the puzzles need to be solved and how they all link together.

This can easily be seen in science too, where students can engage in investigations to discover scientific principles by formulating hypotheses and testing their ideas through experiments using the scientific method. In this process students learn and understand not only the content, but also the scientific process (Piaget, 1972). Additionally, it provides opportunities for a more active involvement in scientific discovery and can create a deeper understanding of the material

(Vygotsky, 1978). Taking students through the process of formulating a hypothesis, then working collaboratively to design and carry out an investigation to test the hypothesis, followed by evaluating the success of their investigations encourages students to think critically about what they are testing and trying to find out and work together to problem-solve how they will effectively test their hypothesis to give accurate and reliable outcomes.

DISCUSSION AND CREATIVE EXPRESSION

The study of languages also benefits from a constructivist approach, especially when activities have a focus that emphasises discussion, collaboration and creative expression. Activities that promote dialogue allow students to share interpretations and encourage them to reflect on their views on text, such as peer-reviewed writing, group projects or literature circles allowing students to develop critical thinking and communication skills, while also constructing their understanding of literature through interaction with their peers (Bruner, 1960). Additionally, allowing students to carry out creative expression exercises in another language – such as creating a story, writing a poem on a specific theme or dialogue between two characters – encourages students to interact with the language in a new and novel way which, in turn, may boost confidence and motivation alongside promoting cultural understanding and supporting emotional expression and adaptability in the language use.

This can also be seen as effective practice in humanities, where, rather than memorising dates and events, encouraging students to explore and discuss primary sources, debate different perspectives and role-play historical figures not only develops critical thinking skills and deepens their understanding, but also allows them to see the relevance of subjects such as history in their own lives. Again, using activities like visual storytelling or historical fictional writing as creative expression helps deepen the understanding students have of human experience. Creating a pretend war diary from the trenches allows them to draw on specific historical knowledge and timelines while enabling them to connect to the people that actually experienced the historical events. Constructivist approaches to learning can allow students to more easily connect with different cultures, philosophies and perspectives, while also giving opportunities for students to strengthen their emotional intelligence through viewing and empathising with different viewpoints and experiences. Both of these may help students develop their own self-confidence and self-identity through the process.

CONSIDER THIS: A TOOL FOR IMPROVING STUDENT ENGAGEMENT

Consider constructivism more as a tool for improving student engagement and motivation over direct learning. In reflecting on this, think about:

- how collaborative learning can be used effectively in the classroom;

- how effective scaffolding can be an effective tool to engage and motivate students;

- how much pre-planning is required for effective constructivist approaches to be used in a lesson.

CHAPTER SUMMARY

Regardless of the specific subject or pedagogical approach, careful planning, particularly in the form of scaffolding, is crucial. This enables a teacher to provide appropriate support and guide students through complex tasks while still fostering student autonomy and ownership of their learning.

When implemented effectively, a hands-on learning approach can lead to both a deeper understanding of content and higher student engagement across all subjects. The applications discussed here represent only a fraction of the possible uses of these principles. It is incumbent upon you as the teacher to identify the strategies that best suit your classroom by blending approaches from the different learning sciences to achieve successful outcomes.

To ensure effectiveness, it is vital to engage in frequent reflection on the purpose and impact of your strategies. Consider the processes and structures you intend to implement to ensure they meet the needs of both you and your students. As with the behaviourist approach and the implementation of any new strategies, it is good professional practice to observe expert practitioners who have already successfully integrated these theories. Focus your attention on their use of enquiry-based learning and how it links to real-world application, as well as on group work, discussions and scaffolding to support student independence in task completion. Consider what elements of other learning sciences they have employed to make their constructivist approaches successful.

These observations can be arranged within your own department, if the practice is already well-established, or with colleagues in other departments where the strategy is more effectively embedded. Starting a dialogue with those in roles that involve frequent observation of teaching practice, such as heads of subject or teaching and learning leads, will help you identify teachers who excel at a given practice and provide the most beneficial observation experiences.

This chapter began by exploring the constructivist approach to learning, focusing on how students actively build their own understanding rather than passively absorbing information. It introduced key theorists, such as Piaget, describing learning as a process in which individuals adapt their mental models through assimilation and accommodation, highlighting the importance of hands-on exploration and problem-solving. Vygotsky's concept of the ZPD was also explored, highlighting the importance of guided learning, where interaction with more knowledgeable peers or teachers supports cognitive growth. The chapter also reviewed Bruner's focus on discovery learning and scaffolding, emphasising the role of structured support in helping learners achieve tasks they might struggle with independently. It used this as a foundation to identify the key principles of constructivism, such as active learning, collaborative learning, scaffolding and contextual learning. However, the chapter warned of the cognitive load generated by unsuccessful discovery learning and how that has influenced those who eschew group work. It further considered the criticisms of constructivism, with some arguing it to be time-consuming and challenging to implement in large classrooms. Kirschner et al. (2006) suggest that minimal guidance methods may overwhelm students lacking foundational knowledge, potentially leading to cognitive overload; lower-achieving students may struggle with independent learning, making structured instruction more effective for certain contexts.

Further development of constructivism was then discussed through Kagan's cooperative learning structures, such as think–pair–share, jigsaw and round robin; these strategies foster student autonomy and engagement and enable deeper comprehension through peer discussions and teamwork.

Finally, the chapter asked you, the reader, to reflect on how you could implement constructivist approaches effectively and encouraged you to consider how constructivist strategies can be adapted to enhance student engagement and learning outcomes.

REFLECTIVE QUESTIONS: CHAPTER 6

Reflect on some of the classes you have taught within the schools where you have worked as a teacher and ask yourself some reflective questions as follows.

Review your department sequences of learning documents and consider how this is underpinned by or deviated from the strategies suggested by the constructivism theory.

- Which strategies support a constructivist approach and which move away from this?

- Do the sequences allow for collaborative learning in the classroom environment?

- Is the learning rooted in real-world contexts?

- Do the sequences provide suitable scaffolding to allow students to be pushed out of their comfort zone and engage in independent learning and critical thinking?

- Are students able to be actively involved in their own learning?

━━ FURTHER READING ━━━━━━━━━━━━━━━━━━━━━━━━━━━━

ITTECF 4.4 Guides, scaffolds and worked examples can help pupils apply new ideas, but should be gradually removed as pupil expertise increases.

Van de Pol, J., Volman, M., Oort, F. and Beishuizen, J. (2015). The effects of scaffolding in the classroom: support contingency and student independent working time in relation to student achievement, task effort and appreciation of support. *Instructional Science, 43*(5), 615–41.

This study by Van de Pol et al. investigates the effectiveness of scaffolding in classrooms, in particular how contingent teacher support effects student achievement, effort and appreciation of support given.

The key findings suggest that scaffolding is not universally beneficial; its effectiveness depends on students' effort and the duration of independent working time. When students worked independently for short periods, low contingent support (frequent, minimal guidance) led to increased achievement and effort. However, when independent working time was longer, high contingent support (tailored, more substantial guidance) proved more effective in increasing achievement while avoiding a sharp decline in task effort.

Additionally, students showed a higher appreciation of teacher support when scaffolding was contingent, reinforcing the importance of personalised assistance. However, task effort generally declined over time, suggesting that students may struggle to maintain engagement without frequent reinforcement.

The study highlights the nuanced impact of scaffolding, showing that the best teaching strategies vary based on classroom dynamics. While scaffolding can enhance learning outcomes, its implementation requires careful balancing of guidance and student autonomy.

── REFERENCES ────────────

Black, P. and Wiliam, D. (1998). Assessment and classroom learning. *Assessment in Education: Principles, Policy and Practice*, 5(1), 7–74.

Bruner, J. S. (1960). *The Process of Education*. Cambridge, MA: Harvard University Press.

Hattie, J. (2009). *Visible Learning: A Synthesis of Over 800 Meta-Analyses Relating to Achievement*. London: Routledge.

Kagan, S. (1994). *Cooperative Learning*. San Clemente, CA: Kagan.

Kirschner, P. A., Sweller, J. and Clark, R. E. (2006). Why minimal guidance during instruction does not work: an analysis of the failure of constructivist, discovery, problem-based, experiential, and inquiry-based teaching. *Educational Psychologist*, 41(2), 75–86.

Piaget, J. (1972). *The Psychology of the Child*. New York: Basic Books.

PISA (2009). *Creating Effective Teaching and Learning Environments: First Results from PISA 2006*. Paris: OECD.

Sweller, J. (1988). Cognitive load during problem solving: effects on learning. *Cognitive Science*, 12(2), 257–85.

Vygotsky, L. S. (1978). *Mind in Society: The Development of Higher Psychological Processes*. Cambridge, MA: Harvard University Press.

7
CONNECTIVISM

INITIAL TEACHER TRAINING AND
EARLY CAREER FRAMEWORK (ITTECF)

The key reading from the ITTECF that we must explore within this chapter is:

Kirschner, P., Sweller, J., Kirschner, F. and Zambrano, J. (2018). From cognitive load theory to collaborative cognitive load theory. *International Journal of Computer Supported Collaborative Learning*, 13(2), 213–33.

INTRODUCTION

This chapter introduces connectivism, a learning theory developed for the digital age by Siemens (2005) and Downes (2005), which posits that traditional learning theories no longer fully account for the profound impact of technology and networked communications on how knowledge is created, accessed and disseminated. It will highlight that learning in the 21st century extends beyond acquiring a static body of knowledge to include navigating, curating and maintaining dynamic connections within vast networks of information. Consequently, this chapter argues that a teacher's role must evolve to equip students with the critical skills to locate, evaluate and synthesise information through various technological means, as this is now as essential as possessing the information itself. We will explore the theoretical underpinnings of connectivism, its urgent practical applications in and beyond the classroom and the key debates and criticisms surrounding this approach, particularly in the context of emerging artificial intelligence (AI).

CONNECTIVISM IN SECONDARY SCHOOLS

It is important to understand that the way we teach in our secondary schools is fundamentally at odds with the world our students are entering. Traditional learning theories, born in a pre-digital era, simply do not account for the seismic shifts brought about by technology and the vast range of networked communications available. The essence of connectivism is not just an interesting academic idea; it is a critical lens for understanding how knowledge is now created, accessed and disseminated. You must accept that learning is more than acquiring a static body of knowledge, it now encompasses navigating, curating and maintaining dynamic connections within a vast network of information (Siemens, 2005). Part of your role as a teacher who uses learning sciences must, therefore, be to equip students with the skills to locate and synthesise information through a myriad and plethora of technological means, as this is now as critical as possessing the information itself.

The unprecedented pace of change and the exponential growth of information, supercharged by powerful AI, demands a new approach. It is no longer sufficient for our students to learn information for a test. They must develop a sophisticated understanding of how to find, evaluate and apply knowledge from diverse, and often conflicting, sources. This isn't a suggestion; it is a necessity. We must urgently cultivate a high level of digital literacy and critical thinking in our classrooms. As a secondary teacher in the UK, this means you must move beyond your reliance on being the main conduit of new knowledge and embrace a more proactive role in facilitating your students' education, empowering them to create and utilise their own *personal learning networks* (PLNs). This chapter is a wake-up call; we will explore the theoretical underpinnings of connectivism, its urgent practical application in your classroom and your students' learning away from school, as well as the key debates and criticisms we must face head-on.

CORE PRINCIPLES THAT MUST GUIDE YOUR PRACTICE

The central tenet of connectivism is that learning occurs in a networked environment, a concept which must permeate your foundational principles. The first of these principles is that learning and knowledge rest in a *diversity* of opinions (Siemens, 2005). In a digital world where information is abundant and often contested, our students are constantly exposed to a multitude of perspectives on any given topic. You must move away from presenting a single, definitive truth. Instead, you must teach students that the process of learning involves critically engaging with this diversity, and that knowledge is fluid and context dependent. This is particularly pertinent for secondary school students who are learning to navigate social media and online spaces, where you must insist they learn to discern fact from opinion and recognise bias. TikTok™ and YouTube™ influencers will affect your students as much as you do – and we do not mean on an entertainment level. We mean on the level of learning – students are accessing online videos as a means of preparing for examinations at an unprecedented level. The voices of those producing online videos are diverse, contradictory and as much right and helpful as they are wrong and counterproductive. Your students have to navigate this maze.

A second key principle that you must embed is that learning is a process of connecting specialised nodes or information sources. These nodes can be anything from a peer in a collaborative project to an academic article, a YouTube tutorial, or an AI tool. Do not underestimate the impact that AI tools have made in terms of being sources of information and especially going forward. Prompt writing and navigating AI tools is a genuine 21st-century skill and the ability to negotiate the world of AI is something that must be taught, rather than learned through *discovery* learning.

The ability to form and maintain all of these connections is not a soft skill; it is a fundamental, non-negotiable skill – a skill which the Turing Report (Aitken et al., 2025) suggests is being utilised by students in independent schools at a greater rate than state secondary schools. Independent schools already dominate examination results and unless you are teaching these connectivist approaches to developing curriculum knowledge and skill any state school students you are teaching will fall further behind. Connectivism enables the learner to draw upon a vast and constantly updated reservoir of knowledge. In your classroom, this must manifest as students using a variety of online resources, such as the BBC Bitesize™ website for revision, the National Archives for a history project and a dedicated subject forum or group to ask a question of a peer. The connections themselves, rather than the information at each node, are what constitute the learning; you need to design your lessons to reflect this learning that takes place beyond your classroom.

Furthermore, you must insist that nurturing and maintaining these connections is needed to facilitate continual learning. The digital world is dynamic; information becomes outdated and new ideas emerge constantly. A learner must be able to adapt and update their PLN to remain current and relevant. If you were a teacher who used to use the Times Educational Supplement Forums for connections, you will have likely migrated to X (formerly Twitter) when the forums closed, using 'Edutwitter' or specific Facebook educational groups. Some teachers then further migrated to Bluesky™, Reddit™ and other online locations when they found X too toxic. Students are navigating similar journeys. They inhabit forums on The Student Room,™ follow specific content providers on YouTube or TikTok and purchase (often with financial support from their parents) access to a vast range of online learning sources – often behind a paywall – that are too vast to list here. This is a critical skill for fostering an attitude of lifelong learning, where education is not something that ends with a final examination or happens purely at a teacher's behest, but a continuous process of engagement with one's network. You must impress upon your students that the skills they develop today must be flexible enough to be applied to future challenges, as they will need to be digitally fluent to thrive in their future careers. The time for passive learning has passed.

Another core skill you must cultivate, according to Siemens (2005), is the ability to see connections between fields, ideas and concepts. Connectivism demands a holistic approach to knowledge, where learning is not confined to isolated subject silos of the sort where it is parcelled up in secondary schools. You must challenge your students to draw a connection between a scientific principle learned in a physics lesson and its application in a design and technology project. This ability to synthesise information across disciplines is not just highly valued; it is essential for solving the complex problems of the modern world. You must actively dismantle the traditional, subject-specific models of learning and encourage a more interdisciplinary curriculum even if the curriculum and examination process of secondary education disincentivises you to do so.

Finally, connectivism asserts that decision-making is itself a learning process. You must teach your students that the veracity of a piece of knowledge may change depending on new information or a shift in context. The act of choosing what to learn and how to learn it is part of the learning journey. The decisions your students make about which sources to trust, what information to prioritise and who to collaborate with are all part of the process of building and refining their understanding. This places a great deal of responsibility on the learner, and it is your job to empower them to take ownership of their educational journey. If a TikTok influencer suggests to them they can 'predict' the precise exam questions they are likely to face, it is your job to pull up that influencer's video in the classroom and deconstruct not only why it is not true, but also what is predictable and who, online, can be relied upon to offer more precise and sensible examination advice. Some elements of examinations are predictable, some questions will be foreseeable cued recall, but some will ask for near and far transfer – as set out in the introduction of this book. Then you can advise how an AI engine can help them with practising that near and far transfer better that any TikTok or YouTuber can.

YOUR ROLE: A TEACHER IN A CONNECTIVIST AND AI-DRIVEN ENVIRONMENT

Connectivism demands a significant re-evaluation of your role as a teacher. The traditional polarised debate between the models of 'sage on the stage' or 'guide by the side' is obsolete. You must become a fusion of both. Your role is not to simply transmit information; it is to also facilitate the connections that allow students to learn aspects of the curriculum or practise recalling or generating near or far transfer for themselves. This requires a new set of pedagogical skills and a fundamentally different approach to curriculum design and delivery. You must be proactive in this transition.

One of your primary responsibilities is network facilitation. This involves helping students to build, manage and critically analyse their digital networks. Students in their teen years are not experts of where reliable online resources can be found, nor are they expert at evaluating sources for veracity or authenticity. You will curate a range of reliable resources to *begin* their enquiry, but, most importantly, you must teach students how to find and evaluate their own sources. This includes providing structured guidance on using search engines effectively, specific AI engines for specific types of learning and remembering, understanding the difference between a primary and a secondary source and recognising the potential biases in online content. You cannot afford to assume they already know how to do this. AI engines habitually hallucinate, online forums contain inaccurate information and misconceptions and TikTok or YouTubers will exaggerate and use hyperbole to attract clicks and subscribers.

This means you have a critical role as a digital curator as well as a teacher. In an environment of information saturation you must act as a filter, highlighting essential resources and helping students to identify the most relevant and trustworthy information. This does not mean dictating what sources students should solely use to learn, but providing a scaffold that prevents them from becoming overwhelmed and which prepares them for continuing their learning once they have left your classroom, either temporarily or forever. For example, a humanities teacher will set up an online area and populate it with reputable links to sources and so forth to enable students and their parents to have a starting place when entering the world of connectivist learning. This is especially important if your students come from a background of low socio-economic status where familial knowledge of education, can, but not always, have limitations.

Some believe that fostering critical media literacy is a skill set that belongs to personal and social health education (PSHE) lessons. And while this is true in terms of the generalist content that features in PSHE lessons, when it comes to subject-specific content of the kind that features in your subject area you should be prepared to supplement that PSHE teaching with a strong steer for your students. In an era of fake news, deepfakes and online manipulation, it is more important than ever to equip students with the skills to be discerning consumers of subject-specific information.

Finally, you must be an active participant in your own learning network, modelling the very behaviour you wish to see in your students. This involves a commitment to professional development, a willingness to experiment with new technologies and a recognition that you, too, are part of a wider community of practice. If you are not learning, you cannot expect your students to either. Exploring and curating nodes of connectivism within your subject will enable you to better broker your students to subject-specific communities of practice and their electronic interactions.

THE FURTHER DEVELOPMENT OF CONNECTIVISM AND AI

The ideas of connectivism have been extended and refined by others, such as Stephen Downes, who focuses on the pedagogical implications of the theory. He emphasises the importance of *massive open online courses* (MOOCs) and the concept of *distributed knowledge* (Downes, 2005). In a connectivist model, knowledge is not centrally held by any one person or institution but is spread across a network. Downes's work highlights the value of peer-to-peer learning and the development of communities of practice where individuals learn from each other through shared interests and collaboration.

In a secondary school context, this can be seen in the use of collaborative online documents and digital forums where students interact with peers. This approach encourages students to be creators as well as consumers of digital content. For example, a Year 10 student could create a YouTube tutorial explaining a mathematical concept or write an authentic wiki-style article on a historical event debasing common misconceptions. The process of creating, sharing and receiving feedback from a wider audience reinforces the principles of network-based learning and fosters a sense of agency and ownership over their work. In a sense, you are enabling your students to operate in the same way that adults in your subject communities operate.

Central to this is the concept of *personal learning environments* (PLEs) and PLNs. A PLE is a self-directed system of resources and tools that a learner uses to manage their own learning. This can include anything from a mind-mapping tool to a social media feed or a dedicated AI-based note-taking application. The PLN, by contrast, is the social network of people and resources that the learner connects with. Your role is to actively help students to build these networks as they get older and closer to leaving your school and, as we repeatedly say, to critically evaluate the quality of the resources and connections within them. This is a crucial skill for lifelong learning, as your students will need to be able to continue to learn and adapt long after they have left their formal education with you or your school.

SUPERCHARGING CONNECTIVISM WITH AI

The advent of artificial intelligence (AI) and machine learning isn't just another technological trend. Instead, it is a new and transformative dimension that will supercharge the core principles of connectivism. AI can be viewed not merely as a tool, but as a new and powerful node within the network, capable of facilitating, personalising and expanding learning in ways previously unimaginable – in particular, through adaptation. This is why the Turing Report (Aitken et al., 2025) found that SEN students were the next most heavy users of AI after independent school students. If you are currently agnostic about AI, then stop viewing AI as a threat and start viewing it as a sophisticated teaching assistant that augments your role as a teacher (Holmes et al., 2021).

One of the most significant contributions of AI is the capacity for personalised learning pathways. Traditional connectivism empowers students to build their own PLNs, but AI can streamline this process by intelligently recommending resources, collaborators and learning experiences tailored to an individual student's needs, interests and prior knowledge. With well-written prompts, the AI-suggested resources can be self-checked for authenticity and veracity. For example, an AI-powered platform could analyse a student's performance in a subject and suggest specific tutorials, articles, or even peer groups to connect with for support, effectively acting as an intelligent network facilitator. This helps to urgently address the challenge of cognitive overload by providing a curated and relevant starting point for every student's enquiry.

Significantly, AI can enhance the development of critical thinking and media literacy, especially related to your subject. AI-driven tools can be trained to help students identify bias in news articles, flag misinformation in online forums and even provide real-time feedback on the coherence and logical fallacies within an argument. In your secondary school context, a student working on a research project could use an AI tool to automatically check the credibility of a source, or to help them structure an essay by identifying weak points in their reasoning or how they have put the essay together structurally. This technology transforms the act of critical evaluation from a purely human process into a collaborative one between student and machine. You should teach them how to use these tools responsibly and effectively – if you are not, other teachers are and thus *your* students will rapidly fall behind those other students.

AI also has the potential to democratise access to expertise and information, thereby helping to mitigate the effects of the digital divide, but, as we have seen from the Turing Report (Aitken et al., 2025), that is not happening – likely because state schools and teachers are not embracing the technology in the same way or at the same speed. While a student in a state school that has limited subject expertise in shortage subjects may struggle to connect with subject matter experts, an AI engine, trained on vast amounts of academic literature, could provide instant, on-demand explanations and answers.

This makes specialised knowledge more accessible to all students, regardless of their geographical location or socio-economic background. It introduces a new type of node to the network – a tireless, always-available source of information that can support your students outside the traditional classroom setting.

You must accept that the integration of AI into connectivist practice, however, is not without its own set of challenges. As a teacher, consider the ethical implications of using AI, including issues of data privacy, algorithmic bias and the potential for over-reliance on technology.

CRITICISMS OF CONNECTIVISM

Despite its compelling vision for learning in the digital age, connectivism has faced several significant criticisms that you should be aware of. A primary argument is that it is not a true learning theory but rather a description of how we use technology to access information. As noted by Kirschner et al. (2006), a theory of learning should explain the internal cognitive processes by which a student actually assimilates and understands information; critics argue that connectivism does not adequately do this and that it focuses more on the external environment and the tools used, rather than the internal mechanisms of the mind. That said, it interfaces and fuses with the other learning theories quite happily: reducing cognitive load, rewarding specific behaviour, helping students to construct new knowledge through constructivism as it facilitates the zone of proximal development (ZPD).

Another critical concern that you must address is the sheer volume of unfiltered information on the internet. Without strong guidance and a solid foundational knowledge base, students can struggle to distinguish between reliable and unreliable sources, which can lead to the spread of misinformation and a lack of critical discernment, as we habitually see at examination time and especially via TikTok. This places an enormous burden on you to equip students with sophisticated subject-specific media literacy skills, a task that can be time-consuming and difficult to embed effectively within an already crowded curriculum. The risk is that a purely connectivist approach could lead to a superficial understanding of a topic, where students are adept at finding information, but lack the foundational knowledge to critically evaluate it.

Furthermore, you must grapple with the persistent issue of the digital divide. Not all students have equal access to technology, reliable internet connections, or the social and cultural capital to build a high-quality PLN. A pedagogical approach that relies heavily on technology and personal networks might inadvertently disadvantage students from less affluent backgrounds or those in rural areas with poor access to technology.

Finally, some teachers argue that connectivism de-emphasises your role as an expert and the importance of direct, explicit instruction. While the theory promotes learner autonomy, there is a risk that foundational knowledge and skills could be overlooked if students are left entirely to their own devices in a digital network. This is particularly relevant in the UK secondary school sector where a core curriculum and national examinations demand a solid grasp of specific, verifiable knowledge. A purely connectivist approach might not be sufficient to ensure students have the depth of understanding required to pass high-stakes examinations. The challenge, therefore, is for you to find the right balance and blend of the different theories of learning – delivering a learner experience that has a balance between a teacher-led, knowledge-rich curriculum and a learner-centred, network-based approach.

CONCLUSION

You will have had personal experience of learning through connectivist nodes in your own development as a secondary subject specialist. You will also have access to communities of practice within and beyond your school. It is good for you to reflect upon how you approach this quite contentious area of learning within your school offer.

PRACTICAL APPLICATION

In your secondary school context, a connectivist approach can be highly effective, particularly in subjects that require the synthesis of information from various sources. It is not about replacing traditional methods entirely, but about urgently integrating new strategies that reflect the nature of how knowledge emerges and is learned in the 21st century.

CONSIDER THIS: CONNECTIVISM

Considering the idea that most approaches to teaching and learning blend ideas from multiple learning sciences, reflect on the idea of connectivism. In reflecting on this, think about the following.

- How can students construct new knowledge without you present?

- Can AI teach your students good study habits?

- Can technology reduce cognitive load and enhance learning?

- How important is it that your specific students learn to socially construct knowledge through technology?

Students can be encouraged to use a variety of digital tools, including search engines, online archives and educational videos on YouTube and TikTok, to gather information and learn. Your role is to provide a framework for critical evaluation, helping students to question a source's origin, its potential bias and its purpose. Here, AI can play a pivotal role. Students should be using an AI tool to rapidly summarise and compare perspectives from multiple online sources, or to create a structured timeline of events from unstructured text (Sørensen and Smedegaard, 2022). The critical point, then, is that students must learn to write prompts that ask AI to teach them the content, to remember the content and to understand how to apply the content to different scenarios in order to promote near and far recall. When they come back to a classroom after learning independently that is an opportunity for teachers like you to evaluate how well they are learning through their technological more capable other.

Where a topic is challenging to learn independently, you can start to prioritise this for classroom-based learning. Where something is quite easy to be undertaken by AI – especially something like retrieval practice which is a study method rather than a teaching method – then you can outsource this to AI.

CHAPTER SUMMARY

This chapter has provided an overview of connectivism, a learning theory developed for the digital age by George Siemens and Stephen Downes. We have explored the theory's core principles, which demand that learning is a network-based activity where knowledge resides in connections rather than in individuals. We have also delved into the significant criticisms surrounding connectivism, including its perceived lack of a robust cognitive framework, the challenges posed by misinformation, the socio-economic implications of the digital divide and the potential for it to undermine the importance of direct instruction and foundational knowledge. It is clear that connectivism is not without its flaws; its wholesale adoption would be irresponsible without careful planning.

However, the practical applications of connectivist strategies, combined with the arrival of the AI age, means that your students risk being left behind if you allow agnosticism to technology to cloud your teaching. By combining the best of traditional pedagogy with a connectivist mindset, you can blend multiple sciences of learning and equip your students with the skills they need to navigate a complex, networked world. The true challenge is for you to find the right balance, ensuring students have a solid foundation of knowledge while also empowering them to become autonomous, lifelong learners who are adept at creating, evaluating and sharing knowledge.

REFLECTIVE QUESTIONS: CHAPTER 7

Can you think of a school- or trust-wide rule or policy that was founded upon an idea or ideas from connectivism?

- What online resources are you expected to provide for students and parents?

- What kinds of online interactions should you be enhancing as part of your teaching?

- How vast is the technological offer in your school? Are you a Chromebook™ school or a more traditional school with little online offer for your students?

- How affluent is the community your school serves? Are you overcoming that with the school offer or are you reinforcing that lack of access?

═══ FURTHER READING ═══════════

ITTECF 4.5 Explicitly teaching pupils metacognitive strategies linked to subject knowledge, including how to plan, monitor and evaluate, supports independence and academic success.

Zimmerman, B. J. (2002). Becoming a self-regulated learner: an overview. *Theory Into Practice, 41*(2), 64–70. https://doi.org/10.1207/s15430421tip4102_2.

This paper provides a clear exploration of self-regulated learning (SRL) and its importance in educational contexts. Zimmerman defines SRL as a process in which learners actively manage the cognitive, motivational and behavioural aspects of their learning. He outlines a cyclical model with three phases: forethought (planning and goal setting), performance (monitoring and control) and self-reflection (evaluating and adjusting strategies). The paper emphasises that SRL helps students compensate for individual differences in learning, promoting autonomy and lifelong learning skills. If you consider the way AI and connected learning networks function and operate then SRL will become an ever more important part of the skill set that learners need to develop in order to excel at learning overall.

═══ REFERENCES ═══════════

Aitken, M., Briggs, M. and Mahomed, S. (2025). *Understanding the Impacts of Generative AI Use on Children: WP2 School-Based Engagements*. London: Alan Turing Institute.

Downes, S. (2005). E-learning 2.0. *eLearn Magazine, 2005*(10).

Holmes, W., Bialik, M. and Fadel, C. (2021). *Artificial Intelligence in Education: A Guide for Teachers and School Leaders*. Boston, MA: Centre for Curriculum Redesign.

Kirschner, P. A., Sweller, J. and Clark, R. E. (2006). Why minimal guidance during instruction does not work: an analysis of the failure of constructivist, discovery, problem-based, experiential, and inquiry-based teaching. *Educational Psychologist, 41*(2), 75–86.

Kirschner, P., Sweller, J., Kirschner, F. and Zambrano, J. (2018). From cognitive load theory to collaborative cognitive load theory. *International Journal of Computer Supported Collaborative Learning, 13*(2), 213–33.

Siemens, G. (2005). Connectivism: A learning theory for the digital age. *International Journal of Instructional Technology and Distance Learning, 2*(1), 3–10.

Sørensen, A. E. and Smedegaard, L. (2022). The role of AI in supporting student engagement and learning in higher education. *Journal of Interactive Learning Research, 33*(3), 257–76.

8

SYNTHESISING THE LEARNING SCIENCES IN THE CLASSROOM AND BEYOND AS A TEACHERS

LEARNING OUTCOMES

By reading this chapter you will develop:

- An understanding of the complex interplay between conflicting learning theories currently popular in English secondary schools
- An understanding of some of the risks of blending learning sciences
- Confidence in using learning sciences to adapt lessons to enable all pupils to participate fully

INITIAL TEACHER TRAINING AND EARLY CAREER FRAMEWORK (ITTECF)

The key reading from the ITTECF that is to be explored within this chapter is:

Kirschner, P., Sweller, J., Kirschner, F. and Zambrano, J. (2018). From cognitive load theory to collaborative cognitive load theory. *International Journal of Computer-Supported Collaborative Learning*, 13(2), 213-33.

INTRODUCTION

This chapter sets out that learning sciences are an integral part of curriculum planning and pedagogical approaches in schools. It highlights that new teachers are introduced to a range of foundational theories, including Vygotsky's social constructivism, Pavlov's and Skinner's behaviourism, Piaget's age-matched learning and Bruner's spiral curriculum, alongside contemporary ideas from cognitivism such as Sweller's cognitive load theory and Baddeley's working memory model. However, the chapter critically notes *cognitive justice* issues within the Initial Teacher Training and Early Career Framework (ITTECF), as it is criticised for its narrow ideological scope, omitting crucial research on neuroscience, neurodiversity and executive function necessary for understanding diverse learning needs. This ideological stance results in varied teacher education experiences and school policies, where theories are often taught and applied in isolation, or policies that appear singular, like SLANT, are in reality a blend of approaches. The chapter argues against this pedagogical tribalism and the false dichotomy between 'traditional' and 'progressive' teaching methods, asserting the need for teachers to develop a comprehensive and blended understanding of learning sciences to avoid exclusionary practices and effectively adapt teaching to the diverse needs of all students

BLENDED LEARNING SCIENCES

Learning sciences are an integral part of how teachers and schools plan their curricula and the pedagogy that they use to deliver that curricula. New teachers in training at universities and schools will be taught about traditional learning sciences such as Vygotsky's (1978) ideas about social constructivist learning, ideas about behaviourism from Pavlov (1927) and Skinner (1953), Piaget's (1952) ideas how learning must be matched to age and sequencing, and Bruner's (1960) ideas on how learning happens through new ideas being constructed with old ideas in a spiral curriculum. This will be supplemented by ideas from cognitivism such as Sweller et al.'s (2019) work on cognitive load theory and Baddeley's (2000) work on working memory. There are also some cognitive justice issues (Shea, 2024) with the learning sciences that new teachers are taught as the ITTECF (DfE, 2019) (the 'entitlement' curriculum stipulated by the DfE in England that all new teachers *must* learn) contains no research from neuroscience and education nor does it feature any research on neurodiversity, children with limited executive control or other areas of research which affect how learning happens. This is a deliberate choice by the authors of the ITTECF because the parameters for the research behind the framework are ideological rather than academic (Hordern and Brooks, 2023).

TEACHER EDUCATION IN HIGHER EDUCATION

Teacher education courses in England run by higher education institutions (HEIs) negate this loss of cognitive justice by teaching ideas beyond the ideological parameters of the ITTECF because of their academic responsibilities under the regulation of the Quality Assurance Agency for Higher Education (QAA). However, not *all* teacher education courses in England do this. Sometimes, the institution delivering teacher education agrees with the ideological position of the DfE and the narrow cognitive parameters of research into learning sciences. These reasons can be financial (some institutions delivering teacher education rely on grants or regular commissions from the DfE) or because those in charge of the institutions are politically motivated to ensure that new teachers emerge with a specific set of ideas matching the research parameters of the ITTECF. This diversity of teacher education experiences matches the diversity of ideas across the landscape of schools and multi-academy trusts (MATs) in England with some trusts adopting the narrow parameters of ideas about learning sciences (and implementing strict non-negotiable trust-wide policies such as suppression of social constructivist learning) and some schools, particularly local authority maintained schools, retaining a degree of autonomy for schools and teachers to adopt learning sciences how they see fit to suit the pupils in their communities.

One tangible issue, which is a theme throughout this book, is that often all of these theories are often taught in isolation and exemplified in isolation. Sometimes new teachers will experience the theories as part of reading secondary texts – such as Lemov's (2015) *Teach Like a Champion* – where they might focus on an exclusive behaviourist approach to learning and teaching. A typical example might be the use of an approach known by its acronym SLANT.

- **S**it up

- **L**isten

- **A**sk and answer questions

- **N**od your head

- **T**rack the teacher

Here we see schools are encouraged to implement this behaviourist approach to all teaching with punitive outcomes for those who do not comply. Yet, in reality, the approach is actually blending a variety of approaches. The term 'listen' actually means to pay attention and draws on Baddeley's model of executive control for content to come together in the working memory. From there, the learning, as Bruner sets out, becomes constructed with pre-existing ideas. Students are asked to 'ask and answer questions', which is socially constructed learning as they move through Vygotsky's ideas about the zone of proximal development (ZPD) with the support of a more capable other – the teacher. The behaviourist ideas of sitting up, nodding the head and tracking the teacher are more about control and cultural mannerisms than about learning sciences. Indeed, a regular criticism is that it treats all pupils and their learning as the same. Some neurodiverse pupils may intensely dislike making eye contact. It also ignores ideas about learning sciences from psychology which look at the importance of 'effort' to learning and the need to understand that effort includes motivation and focus as well as intrinsic task difficulty. However, new teachers reading Lemov's book or training in a school that has decided to use the book as their ideological approach to teaching and learning will not necessarily be learning the nuances and theories behind such simplistic policies or their limitations. They may learn that so-called 'behaviourist' approaches to teaching and learning are not only 'traditional' but also superior to 'progressive' ideas about teaching and learning which rely upon ideas such as social constructivism.

LEARNING SCIENCES 'WARS'

There is no escaping that in England there has been conflict between those who feel that a fusion of behaviourism and cognitivism is the way teaching and learning should take place (traditional) and those who feel that such a narrow parameter of ideas is exclusionary (progressive). Yet, the reality is both sides blend all the learning sciences within their teaching and learning to a variety of degrees. And there is also a strong need for teachers to have a strong understanding of not just each learning science, but also a body of research into how learning science has been turned into teaching (for learning sciences are not teaching sciences), the blending that has taken place and, finally, the exclusionary limitations that this lack of knowledge leads to. Attendance at schools in England has been falling year on year since students returned from the COVID-19-era lockdowns (DfE, 2024). While the reasons behind these are multifaceted and complex, the way learning sciences inform teaching and learning in English schools is currently quite ideological rather than comprehensively evidence- and research-informed. Learning sciences can and must be used in an inclusionary way. Creating rigid school policies based on limited, sometimes incorrect understanding of learning sciences will affect a subset of children and their learning experience; this is something that needs to be improved.

PRE-LESSON ADAPTATION AND IN-LESSON ADAPTATION

The first premise of blending learning sciences is to understand that, unlike the heading in Standard 2 of the ITTECF 'How pupils learn', learning sciences cannot speak for all pupils. Deaf pupils will 'listen' differently to hearing pupils; vision-impaired pupils will ask and answer questions differently to sighted pupils; and so forth. Indeed, the level and quality of provision for such pupils will vary for each pupil, depending on a few factors. The first question a teacher should reflect upon is whether they need to undertake pre-lesson adaptation for any of their pupils. They must understand the learning sciences that are to be used in the lesson and then make the adaptations necessary to maximise the inclusionary nature of their lesson. This means autonomy to adapt school-wide 'non-negotiables' as they see fit.

Further, embracing the idea that all humans are 'neurodiverse' to one degree or the other, a teacher must adapt in-lesson depending on pupil need. A dehydrated pupil or a hungry pupil may not be able to pay attention as the policy states. They might be able to pretend to listen, but an experienced teacher needs to be able to adapt within lesson. The school may have bought in a curriculum written by an external person and be delivering it to the class regardless of inconsistent pre-existing knowledge. The teacher needs the autonomy to adapt the curriculum to match the pupils in front of them to ensure the constructivist experience is positive and inclusionary. This can happen at a single-pupil level or at whole-class level. Teachers need to be able to undertake in-lesson adaptation according to their continuous assessment of the class.

CONCLUSION

Rigid or ideological adherence to teaching and learning policies based on an understanding (or otherwise) of learning sciences will always lead to an exclusionary experience for some pupils. Each pupil has an entitlement to learn well and to have their learning enhanced by their teacher's strong knowledge of learning sciences and ability to adapt the learning experience for their pupils.

PRACTICAL APPLICATION

CONSIDER THIS: GROUP LEARNING

Considering the idea that most approaches to teaching and learning blend ideas from multiple learning sciences; reflect on the idea of 'group learning'. In reflecting on this, think about:

- how behaviourism is central to good group work;

- how new knowledge is constructed from group work that could not exist without the social interaction;

- how cogntivism is vital to understanding what good group work is;

- the pre-lesson and in-lesson adaptation you have had to make to ensure group work is a positive experience for all pupils.

Understanding the theoretical concepts of the learning science is important to be able to implement these strategies in the classroom. However, having consideration for how they can be implemented in the classroom is also key.

If we take the theory of social constructivism, as an example, probably when you consider implementing these concepts your thoughts instantly go to group work, quickly followed by observation of bad practices when implementing group work. I'm sure you have seen, countless times, a teacher instructing a class to get into 'groups of their choice', give the instructions for the activity or task and then sit back and let it descend into what could be considered unstructured chaos – then, after the group activity, being frustrated that the class has not achieved what they were expecting them to. This is often why group work is shied away from in many classroom environments, with a preference for independent study, often in silence. However, group work can be a very impactful tool in supporting the learning of students if implemented effectively and there are certain subjects where this tool is almost a necessity to the learning of students – such as practical work in science, team games in PE, choral work in music and performance work in drama. Each of these subjects has group work as a core of their teaching philosophy and must ensure that they are implementing this effectively. Rarely do you see a teacher of science, PE, music, or drama let students form groups and just get on with it. No; they will often carefully cultivate the learning environment to ensure that every member of the group is supported and has a key role to play in the group activity.

If we look at Year 7s lighting a Bunsen burner in science, for example, this would generally be done in pairs. Often they will be paired with someone they feel comfortable with; using fire can be quite daunting to an 11-year-old who has had little to no experience of practical science. Each student in the pair can be given a role description – like 'fire starter' and 'Bunsen buddy', or simply 'Person A' and 'Person B' (but that's a little less fun). They would then take it in turns to light the splint, take it to the Bunsen burner, turn on the gas tap, change the flame type and then turn off the gas tap. Each student has a clear understanding of their role and the importance of their role, thus effectively learning how to safely light a Bunsen burner.

Another example of a similar structure can be implemented in drama. Groups can be carefully selected to ensure they have a mix of: a strong director, to take ideas and guide others on how to deliver them; strong performers, who are more willing to take larger roles and support others with their performance; and technician, who can look at things more technically, such as set and staging, to maximise effect to the audience. This allows them to work more easily to their strengths and support each other in developing the skills they are perhaps less able in. In addition, assigning these roles to students in groups (and not necessarily due to their natural ability in them) will give individuals a clear focus in their role, therefore encouraging more active involvement. Another role which can be given to students who are unwilling to perform is the role of critic, where they must watch and feed back on the performance with what was effective and what needs developing further.

Modelling is another practical tool which can be effectively implemented in the classroom, this time to support cognitive load and theory. Modelling can come in many formats such as: the modelling of a specific technique in PE, DT, art or drama; a practical investigation in science; the writing or analysis of a poem or script in English; how you solve a problem in maths; or even how to use a program in computer science. There are countless ways to use this technique, however; what is important is that it is far more than just showing and telling the students what to do.

Let take modelling the drawing of a graph in maths or science as an example. First, ensuring all students can see the modelling example is crucial; this can often be done most effectively when projecting onto the board using a visualiser. Replicating exactly the process they will be carrying out – including resources, such as the paper they are to use – will be more successful than the students trying to process the conversion of a different-scaled model being draw on the board; the former is already lowering their cognitive load. Second, as you move through the steps the students are to carry out – drawing axis, choosing scales, plotting points and so on – a decision needs to be made whether they are to follow along in real time, step by step, or complete the task after the modelling. Both have their benefits: the first reduces the cognitive load further as the students can focus on one step at a time, but can become more time-consuming, requiring all students to complete work at a similar pace; the second allows students to complete the task at their own pace and allows the teacher to provide additional support to individual students where needed, but increases the cognitive load as students must be able to recall and act upon a series of steps in one process. Once this decision is made, regardless of which approach is taken, it is vital that the modelling is punctuated with questions – both descriptive 'what am I doing?' questions and explanatory 'why am I doing it?' questions. This not only supports active engagement of the students during the modelling, but also allows them to actively process and develop understanding of the process. Finally, once the modelling is done, students need opportunities to apply what they have learned independently to embed the practice and skills. In the example of drawing graphs, this can be done by simply providing similar data sets for them to draw graphs from. You may be able to slightly increase the level of the independent practice, such as using a slightly more challenging scale, but you should avoid independent learning that is significantly different from the modelling exercise without additional modelling taking place – such as plotting into the negative or plotting multiple data sets – as this will significantly increase the cognitive loading on the student, leading to them becoming frustrated with the task and thus less willing to engage. Additionally, a balance needs to be struck between deciding to model and not; always modelling can lead to students becoming dependent on this, decreasing their ability to think independently or their willingness to make mistakes in their practice.

Obviously, there are a multitude of avenues for practical applications that can be looked at when considering how to implement learning theories in practice in the classroom. Hopefully, the examples outlined above allow you to start considering ways you can use these theories in your own subjects and practice. Make sure you always: reflect on and identify the intended purpose of the activity; carefully consider processes and structures you are going to put in place to ensure the activity is completed by the students as you desire; understand and rationalise the purpose and effectiveness of the activity in ensuring positive outcomes and student progress. A good starting point and good professional practice when you want to try a new idea or activity in your classroom is, when possible, to observe expert others where this practice is already effectively embedded in their own teaching. This can be in department, if is it is already common practice, or out of department, if it is known that that strategy is more effectively embedded elsewhere. Simply opening a conversation with colleagues whose role is to more frequently to observe practice in your department or across the school, such as heads of subject or departments or teaching and learning leads, will help you identify teachers who excel at a given practice for you to seek guidance from. Alternatively, it might highlight a gap in the skill set of the department or school as a whole which could lead to opportunities for you to explore, research, develop and share good practice yourself. At the end of the day, if you don't ask and you don't try, you won't know and you won't learn.

CHAPTER SUMMARY

The aim of this chapter was to stimulate your thinking about how the learning sciences can be synthesised and used in a blended way to support learning. As we have seen, there are a variety of learning theories which can and should be used to support our decisions when planning the learning activities within our lessons. Whether planning new material from scratch, or adapting already existing resources, in order to ensure an equitable experience for all we should feel empowered to make adaptations within lessons based upon the responses of the pupils in front of us. A sound knowledge of the key tenets of the learning sciences will enable us to support our pupils' learning to the best effect, confident in the knowledge that we are using the correct approach for those pupils in that lesson. It is important to remember that we may change approaches depending on the class or even the time of day, and we will never teach any one lesson in the same way. All of this is underpinned by good assessment for learning (AfL), where teachers use information about student achievement to make adjustments throughout the lesson (Wiliam, 2017). We are vigilant to the reactions of the pupils and may change tack part way through based on their responses to questions and activities.

We have seen that there exists a false dichotomy between the so-called 'traditional' approach to teaching, which includes direct instruction and strictly held behaviourist approaches, and the so-called 'progressive' approaches, which include opportunities for social constructivist methods and a more dialogic way of teaching. The reality is that there is a continuum of approaches that the skilled teacher can choose from, depending on the situation, the individual pupils, the activity and the intended learning goals. Often, a period of behaviourist-driven direct instruction is necessary if you are teaching pupils new knowledge or skills, before they are able to begin to form their own opinions and discuss various possibilities in a social constructivist way. Activating their pre-existing schema by bringing similar experiences or linked situations to the fore before introducing the new learning will better enable them to commit the new learning to the long-term memory and begin the formation of new schema, while reducing the cognitive load required to grapple with completely new concepts. Modelling by an expert other and opportunities to practise new skills before moving on will help to consolidate the learning, but it will need to be revisited several times before it becomes fully embedded and accessible to the working memory.

It is clear that by using a blend of learning sciences we are likely to achieve optimum learning for our pupils; however, it is also important to recognise the importance of getting all the elements right. If one part is done badly, the others will suffer. A good example is the currently popular notion of carrying out retrieval practice of prior learning at the beginning of lessons. Based on theories of memory developed by Roediger and Butler (2011), the suggestion is that by revisiting learning from days or weeks earlier, through the act of retrieval, our memory for that information is strengthened and forgetting is less likely to occur. However, if done badly, this retrieval practice can result in the activation of schemata (Piaget, 1952) that are inappropriate to the upcoming lesson. This could have the effect of causing extraneous load on the working memory and lead to confusion about the new learning.

Schemas (or schemata) are an abstract concept that propose units of understanding that create a web of complex relationships with one another. Where new information is attached to existing schemata, the easier it is to remember it. Importantly, new information will not attach to existing schemas if pupils are not already thinking about that schema when the information comes in – for example, if they are still thinking about other topics which have been revisited during retrieval practice. Schema theory is also useful when we come to think about creating opportunities for social constructivist learning. How can we be sure that all pupils have the necessary schemata in order to participate fully?

Social constructivist learning in the form of group work is perhaps the form of pedagogy that is fraught with most difficulties when it comes to blending learning sciences. Expectations for successful group work need to be set up correctly and tightly controlled using behaviourist techniques at the outset. Pupils will need to have had some degree of direct instruction prior to being able to work together and, in order for the task to be successful, there must be a clear articulation of individual roles, expected group outcomes and pupil motivation to complete the task to a good standard, within the time allocated. To facilitate successful group work, we must also have a clear understanding of social dynamics in collaborative learning approaches, otherwise some pupils may be reluctant to participate and prefer to work on their own. Knowledge of theories of motivation, self-confidence and self-efficacy will enable teachers to better support pupils engaging in collaborative learning activities. Additionally, it is important to allow all pupils the opportunity to talk and articulate their thinking during collaborative tasks to ensure they benefit equally from the positive impact that practice at communication with peers can bring them. Here it is clear that an understanding of dialogic approaches to teaching is also beneficial; Alexander (2020) discusses the power of talk to engage students' interest, stimulate their thinking, advance their understanding and expand their ideas.

It makes sense that it is easier to talk about learning with pupils if there is a shared common language and they are able to talk to their teachers using terms that everyone understands. Using correct terms when talking about learning sciences and classroom practice can develop pupils' understanding of metacognition, which is the process by which learners use knowledge of the task at hand, knowledge of learning strategies and knowledge of themselves to plan their learning, monitor their progress towards a learning goal and then evaluate the outcome.

REFLECTIVE QUESTIONS: CHAPTER 8

Reflect on some of the classes you have taught within the schools where you have worked as a teacher and ask yourself some reflective questions as follows.

Can you think of a school- or trust-wide rule or policy that was founded upon an idea or ideas from a learning science?

- What situations did that rule of policy help with?

- Can you recall incidents where the rule of policy was inappropriate for an individual learner?

- Did you have autonomy to ignore or adapt the rule to be inclusionary?

- Do you have an anecdote or example of where you have seen something positive happen because of the inclusionary approach of a teacher?

- Do you have an anecdote or example of where a pupil's learning experience was hampered by rigid adherence to a narrow rule or policy?

FURTHER READING

ITTECF 4.9 Paired and group activities can increase pupil success, but to work together effectively pupils need guidance, support and practice.

Kirschner, P., Sweller, J., Kirschner, F. and Zambrano, J. (2018). From cognitive load theory to collaborative cognitive load theory. *International Journal of Computer-Supported Collaborative Learning, 13*(2), 213–33.

Kirschner et al. suggest that when pupils work collaboratively they learn through imitation, listening to each other and reading others' ideas. Problem-solving strategies are tested through trial and error. Additionally, in the process of collaborating, learning is facilitated by a *collective working memory effect*, as pupils collectively process new information. This can be conceived as a shared working memory that combines and connects the knowledge (schema) held in the working memory of each individual, which reduces their own cognitive load and enables greater success in solving more complex problems or completing more intricate tasks than the individual could on their own.

However, the demands on cognitive load will be increased if members of a group have not worked together before or do not know how to work together in a given context, which will have a negative impact on their learning. Group members will need guidance and support in being able to share knowledge and information efficiently. Assigning roles and providing worked examples can support the collaborative process. Kirschner et al. suggest a number of principles specific to the design of collaborative learning which take into account the possibilities and limitations of collaborative cognitive load theory which will help teachers to make informed decisions that will increase the chances of the learning goals being met.

━━ REFERENCES ━━━━━━━━━━━━━━━━━━━━━━━━━━━━

Alexander, R. (2020). *A Dialogic Teaching Companion.* London: Routledge.

Baddeley, A. (2000). The episodic buffer: a new component of working memory? *Trends in Cognitive Sciences,* 4(11), 417–23.

Bruner, J. (1960). *The Process of Education.* Cambridge, MA: Harvard University Press.

Department for Education (DfE) (2019). *Initial Teacher Training (ITT): Core Content Framework.* Available at: www.gov.uk/government/publications/initial-teacher-training-itt-core-content-framework. Accessed 20 November 2025.

DfE (2024). *Pupil Absence in Schools in England.* Available at: https://explore-education-statistics.service.gov.uk/find-statistics/pupil-absence-in-schools-in-england. Accessed 20 November 2025.

Hordern, J. and Brooks, C. (2023). The Core Content Framework and the 'new science' of educational research. *Oxford Review of Education,* 49(1), 1–19.

Kapur, R. (2018). The significance of social constructivism in education. Unpublished manuscript, University of Delhi.

Kirschner, P., Sweller, J., Kirschner, F. and Zambrano, J. (2018). From cognitive load theory to collaborative cognitive load theory. *International Journal of Computer-Supported Collaborative Learning,* 13(2), 213–33.

Lemov, D. (2015). *Teach Like a Champion 2.0.* Hoboken, NJ: John Wiley & Sons.

Pavlov, I. P. (1927). *Conditioned Reflexes: An Investigation of the Physiological Activity of the Cerebral Cortex.* Oxford: Oxford University Press.

Piaget, J. (1952). *The Origins of Intelligence in Children.* Madison, CT: International Universities Press.

Roediger, H. L. and Butler, A. C. (2011). The critical role of retrieval practice in long-term retention. *Trends in Cognitive Sciences,* 15(1), 20–7.

Shea, J. (2024). How reforms of teacher education challenge principles of social justice. In **J. Wearmouth, U. Maylor, K. Lindley and J. Shea** (eds), *Social Justice in Education.* New York: McGraw Hill, pp. 39–55.

Sweller, J., Merriënboer, J. and Paas, F. (2019). Cognitive architecture and instructional design: 20 years later. *Educational Psychology Review,* 31, 261–92.

Vygotsky, L. (1978). *Mind in Society: The Development of Higher Psychological Processes.* Cambridge, MA: Harvard University Press.

Wiliam, D. (2017). *Embedded Formative Assessment,* 2nd edn. Bloomington, IN: Solution Tree.

PART 3

PART 3

9

HOW LEARNING SCIENCES INFLUENCE CURRICULUM DESIGN AND SEQUENCING

LEARNING OUTCOMES

By reading this chapter you will develop:

- An understanding of the principles of effective curriculum design and sequencing
- An understanding of how learning sciences can be used to inform curriculum planning
- An understanding of how to interrogate pre-written lesson plans so that you may adapt them confidently for your own students

INITIAL TEACHER TRAINING AND EARLY CAREER FRAMEWORK (ITTECF)

The key reading from the ITTECF that is to be explored within this chapter is:

Biesta, G. (2009). Good education in an age of measurement: on the need to reconnect with the question of purpose in education. *Educational Assessment, Evaluation and Accountability, 21*(1), 33–46. https://doi.org/10.1007/s11092-008-9064-9

INTRODUCTION

This chapter will provide a comprehensive overview of how learning sciences influence curriculum design and sequencing. It explores key principles of effective curriculum design, which is the intentional planning of what, when and how students learn, and sequencing, the logical organisation of content to promote cumulative understanding and reduce cognitive overload. The chapter integrates insights from various learning sciences, including cognitivism, behaviourism, constructivism and connectivism, to show how they can inform curriculum planning and are applied in practice. Additionally, it addresses the critical perspective of Biesta (2009: 36) on the 'learnification' of education and his framework of *qualification, socialisation* and *subjectification* to reconnect with the deeper purpose of education beyond what is simply measurable. The chapter also aims to equip you with the knowledge to critically evaluate and adapt existing lesson plans to suit your students' needs.

Curriculum design refers to the intentional planning of what pupils learn, when they learn it and how learning builds over time, while sequencing is the process of organising content so that it progresses logically and supports cumulative understanding. Effective sequencing ensures that pupils can connect new knowledge to prior learning, reducing cognitive overload and promoting retention. Curriculum design and sequencing benefit greatly from insights drawn from multiple learning sciences. Rather than relying on a single theoretical approach, effective curriculum planning integrates principles from cognitivism, behaviourism, constructivism and connectivism, each offering distinct contributions to how content is organised and delivered.

CURRICULUM DESIGN AND SEQUENCING IN SECONDARY SCHOOLS

In England, curriculum design is shaped by national frameworks, subject-specific guidance and school- or trust-level decisions. Teachers play a vital role in interpreting, adapting and implementing curriculum plans, ensuring that lessons are coherent, purposeful and responsive to pupil needs. Typically, in England, secondary school curricula are organised into separate subjects, or disciplines. Organising the curriculum this way can make it more manageable, and each subject is seen to have its own disciplinary knowledge, as well as particular skills and pedagogies associated with it. However, this predisposition to treat subjects as separate from each other can be problematic. As Unwin and Yandell (2017: 75) remind us, school subjects are 'shifting and unstable domains' – for example, geography cannot be easily separated from disciplines like history, science, economics, or politics. In addition, the separation of subjects discourages students from making connections between their learning in different areas of the curriculum (Unwin and Yandell, 2017) which, as we have seen from Chapter 5 in this book, is a skill that will support the formation of schemata for newly encountered topics.

The separation of curricula into separate subjects also means that the national government have the power to decide what is to be taught by implementing a national curriculum for most subjects (drama, most notably, does not have a national curriculum document), at Key Stage 3 and Key Stage 4, which government-funded state schools are or will be mandated to follow (academies and free schools currently have freedom not to follow national curricula, but legislation in the form of the Children's Wellbeing and Schools Act is due which will remove this freedom). Senior school or trust leaders will interpret the national curriculum, and subject leaders must demonstrate in their long-term plans how it is to be delivered. Long-term plans, which map what a class might cover across a year or key stage, are typically broken down into medium-term plans, which are organised into sequence of lessons over a unit of work. These typically last for half a term and are punctuated by assessment points. The daily lesson plans that make up the sequences can also be known as short-term plans.

Bruner (1966) proposed a spiral approach to curriculum design, suggesting that complex ideas can be introduced at a simplified level then revisited with increasing levels of complexity and depth at later stages. The idea is that pupils return to important ideas at multiple points in their education, each time gaining a deeper and more sophisticated understanding (Bruner,1966). This approach to sequencing can often be seen in the subject long-term plans, where concepts introduced in Year 7 are revisited and built upon in Year 8 and subsequent years; however, experienced teachers are often dismayed when students deny all knowledge of a topic that the teacher knows they have been taught in previous years. Cognitivist principles of learning demonstrate that if pupils have not been required to actively bring the information to mind in the intervening period, they are likely to struggle to access the memories of it when the topic is reintroduced many months later (Dunlosky et al., 2013). Thus, when designing the curricula it is important to bear in mind that medium- and short-term plans must include opportunities for retrieval practice of previously learned materials.

In addition to the requirements of the subject national curriculum, there are many other pressures on curriculum design in secondary schools in England. Most notably, there is the need to ensure that students are fully prepared for the demands of GCSEs and A levels. When designing the long-term plans, subject leaders will often work backwards from these examinations, to ensure that students have ample opportunity to develop and consolidate the knowledge and skills they will need to be successful in the examinations. However, this approach risks narrowing the Key Stage 4 curriculum as it might become examination-focused, with students only being exposed to what is necessary to pass the exams and not experiencing the wider subject matter.

To combat this narrowing of the curriculum, it is argued that the Key Stage 3 curriculum offers greater opportunities for flexibility in teaching aspects of the subject that will be most beneficial to students, in the hope of engendering a love of the subject and the joy of learning. Key Stage 3 is not constrained by the requirements of the GCSE exams, so teachers have more choice about what to include. However, as Unwin and Yandell (2017) point out, designing a curriculum involves making choices about what is excluded too, as well as potentially making decisions about what is appropriate for some students and not others. Every curriculum reflects underlying beliefs about values and intentions, including what knowledge is considered important, which skills are deemed essential and, ultimately, the purpose of education itself. These decisions will be guided by the school ideology and the philosophy of the teachers delivering the lessons.

A major criticism of curriculum design and content in England is that the content taught does not always reflect the profile of the students, in that the achievements and contributions to the subject by women and people of working class or minority ethnic origins can go uncommented on. From a constructivist perspective, this means some students will construct new knowledge more readily than others. This can lead to students not relating to subjects as they think this subject is 'not for people like me'. Subject leaders might want to bring in new content to address these inequalities, but depleted school budgets often mean there are not the financial resources available to buy new texts or equipment that properly reflect their students' profiles and interests. Instead, individual teachers must ensure the curriculum recognises the contributions to the subject of all sections of society and, if they are not visible, to encourage students to notice and ask why this is.

New pre-service teachers will typically begin their school practice by teaching small episodes of lessons, moving on to whole lessons, then onto teaching sequences of learning. Initially, the teaching of discrete lessons or parts of lessons can be a supportive strategy in terms of helping new teachers to develop their behaviourist strategies for managing the unfamiliar classroom environment and learning the names of their pupils, as well as helping them to manage their own potential cognitive overload as they try to remember all the new and unfamiliar routines, the behaviour policy and the subject knowledge they are trying to impart. However, pre-service teachers typically report that they find teaching sequences is often easier than stand-alone lessons, as they know what the students have already studied, have identified some misconceptions that they will need to go back and review, and know what the final outcomes of the sequence will be. This fits with what you have learned about cognitive science, in terms of extraneous load, and also from constructivism – as students need to construct new knowledge into foundational knowledge.

Additionally, as they develop automaticity in the managing the behaviourist structures of the classroom – such as knowing the students' names and the behaviour policy – the teaching of pre-service teachers improves along with their confidence and ability to 'think outside the box' when it comes to dealing with unexpected questions or the ubiquitous wasp that will disrupt even the most well-ordered of classrooms (there is no more extraneous load than an extraneous wasp!). As can be seen, the theories of learning that have been discussed in this book can be applied to pre-service teachers as well as to their students in the classroom.

CORE PRINCIPLES OF CURRICULUM DESIGN AND SEQUENCING

Effective curriculum design and sequencing integrate principles from all the learning sciences, each offering distinct yet complementary contributions to how content is organised and delivered. Below is a summary of the contributions that each learning science can make to curriculum design, and teachers should feel empowered to use different aspects from all the learning sciences at different times, depending on the subject, the topic to be taught and the needs of the students they have in front of them. This integrated approach ensures that curriculum is not only coherent and cumulative, but also responsive to how pupils learn best.

BEHAVIOURISM

Behaviourism focuses on observable behaviours, routines and reinforcement, positing that behaviour is learned through conditioning and responses to environmental stimuli. The curriculum should embed clear routines with a focus on immediacy, frequency and consistency. This includes prompt starts to lessons and do now tasks, creating a clear routine for the start of a lesson. It promotes desired learning behaviours through positive reinforcement (such as precise praise and reward systems) to foster accomplishment and a strong work ethic, while sanctions or removal of merits can provide further reinforcement of expected behaviours. Although behaviourism is best seen as a tool for improving student engagement and motivation to participate, rather than a learning method itself (retrieval practice notwithstanding), behaviourist principles contribute to curriculum design by focusing on observable outcomes and reinforcement. While behaviourism may not address deeper understanding, it supports the development of foundational skills and routines, especially in early stages of learning. Behaviourist strategies can also support direct instruction, as the established behaviourist routines help to ensure that students are paying attention to the teacher's exposition.

Behaviourism's contribution to curriculum sequencing includes:

- clear learning objectives which define measurable outcomes for each unit or lesson;

- assessment-driven sequencing, aligning curriculum progression with performance benchmarks and mastery checks;

- sequencing involving the repetition of skills and knowledge tasks to facilitate learning through practice to strengthen desired behaviours, skills or automated cued retrieval of specific knowledge such as times tables;

- structured transitions with clear signals (e.g., a 3–2–1 countdown) and specific instructions which allow consistent application of reinforcement;

- school behaviour policies often underpinning sequencing, starting with positive or negative reinforcement and reinforcing routines for learning, and allowing for uninterrupted teacher exposition.

COGNITIVISM

Cognitivism views learning as an internal process of acquiring, organising and storing information, likening the mind to a computer. It focuses on how students process information, develop mental representations (schemas) and retrieve knowledge from memory. Instruction must be designed to avoid overloading working memory by minimising distractions, ensuring content is focused and presenting information efficiently across sensory channels (for example, through dual coding). The curriculum should be designed to help students build and strengthen mental frameworks (schemas) by connecting new information meaningfully with prior knowledge. This means actively accessing relevant existing schemas. It should also integrate metacognitive techniques and self-regulated learning (SRL), where students plan, monitor and evaluate their own learning strategies. In addition, curriculum designers should foster positive emotional states, as emotion and cognition are integrated and enhance engagement and memory consolidation.

Cognitivism's contribution to curriculum sequencing includes:

- incorporating regular retrieval practice (e.g., low-stakes quizzes, flashcards) to strengthen memory and improve long-term retention;

- sequencing content, revisiting through spaced learning (distributing study time) to boost storage strength and long-term retention;

- interleaving, mixing different but related topics, should be used to force the brain to work harder, strengthening learning and discerning similarities;

- presenting information using both verbal and visual channels (dual coding), such as diagrams with explanations, to distribute cognitive load and create stronger memory traces;

- breaking down complex content into manageable sections (chunking) and providing temporary scaffolding that is gradually removed;

- beginning lessons with tasks that activate relevant prior knowledge (e.g., do now tasks) to link new learning to existing schemas and reduce cognitive load.

CONSTRUCTIVISM

Constructivism emphasises the active role of students in building their own understanding through experiences and interactions, rather than passively receiving information. Adding constructivist strategies to curriculum design will provide a comprehensive approach to fostering effective and engaging learning experiences. The curriculum should promote active learning, where students are involved through exploration, problem-solving and enquiry. It advocates for collaborative learning, seeing it as a social activity where students work together to share knowledge and solve problems. Kagan's cooperative structures like think–pair–share, jigsaw and round robin are examples that foster peer interaction and active participation. Lessons should be rooted in real-world contexts to make learning meaningful, allowing students to apply concepts in practical situations, such as by including budgeting in maths or historical role-play in humanities. Curriculum design should also encourage self-evaluation and critique, especially in subjects like art, English literature, drama and physical education, valuing the learning process over the outcome. In constructivist pedagogies, the teacher's role is primarily that of a facilitator, guiding students in achieving learning outcomes and supporting their autonomy. Strategies for critical thinking and problem-solving should be integrated, such as through enquiry-based experiments in science, where students might formulate hypotheses and test ideas. Discussion and creative expression should be encouraged through dialogue, peer-reviewed writing and creative projects, which are seen to deepen understanding and promote cultural awareness.

Constructivism's contribution to curriculum sequencing includes:

- providing suitable scaffolding within the curriculum – that is, temporary support that helps students achieve tasks they cannot accomplish alone, gradually removing it as competence increases;

- sequencing to allow students to build on their prior knowledge and personal experiences, as learning is seen as deeply personal and contextual;

- activities being sequenced to push students through their zone of proximal development (ZPD) (Vygotsky, 1978) – that is, the space between independent ability and what can be achieved with assistance;

- promoting progression from exploring and questioning to critical thinking and deeper understanding;

- learning sequences progressively involving students in formulating their own strategies and solutions, moving them towards greater independence;

- sequencing to allow for collaborative activities where more capable peers support less confident students, supporting deeper understanding for both sets of students.

CONNECTIVISM

Connectivism posits that learning occurs in a networked environment, where knowledge resides in connections within a vast network of information, rather than solely within individuals. It is crucial for equipping students for the digital age. Curriculum should embrace diverse opinions and networked learning, moving away from a single truth, teaching students to critically engage with multiple perspectives and seeing knowledge as fluid and context dependent. As such, learning is designed as a process of connecting specialised nodes or information sources, which can include peers, academic articles, YouTube tutorials, or AI tools. It insists on nurturing and maintaining these connections to facilitate continual and lifelong learning, enabling students to adapt and update their personal learning networks (PLNs). Curriculum design should empower students to take ownership of their educational journey by teaching that decision-making about what to learn, how to learn and which sources to trust is part of the learning process. An interdisciplinary approach is encouraged, challenging students to draw connections between fields, ideas and concepts across subjects to solve complex modern problems. AI should be integrated as a powerful 'node' to enable personalised learning pathways, recommend resources, enhance critical thinking (e.g., bias identification) and democratise access to specialised knowledge.

Connectivism's contribution to curriculum sequencing includes:

- explicit teaching of skills to find, evaluate and synthesise information from diverse online sources, including structured guidance on using search engines, specific AI engines and recognising biases;

- progressively helping students build, manage and critically analyse their PLNs and personal learning environments (PLEs) as they mature;

- encouraging students to transition from consumers to creators of digital content (e.g., YouTube tutorials, wiki articles), reinforcing network-based learning and agency;

- prioritising challenging topics for classroom-based learning, while outsourcing more routine tasks, such as retrieval practice, to AI tools;

- evolution of the teacher's role to facilitate student connections, curate reliable resources and model participation in professional learning networks, guiding students through the complexities of online information.

BLENDING LEARNING SCIENCES FOR COMPREHENSIVE CURRICULUM DESIGN

While each theory has its strengths, limitations exist – for example, behaviourism removing agency; cognitivism's narrow focus; constructivism's resource demands; and connectivism's challenges with misinformation. Therefore, a blended approach is most effective for an optimum learning environment.

Curriculum design and sequencing, therefore, should:

- utilise behaviourist principles to establish clear routines, manage the learning environment and motivate students through consistent reinforcement and clear expectations, providing a structured foundation. These aspects of behaviourism underpin successful classroom management and will support direct instruction and teacher exposition, as well as constructivist and connectivist pedagogies;

- employ cognitivist strategies to ensure information is processed effectively, reducing cognitive load, building robust mental schemas and enhancing memory through techniques like retrieval practice, spaced learning, interleaving and dual coding;

- integrate constructivist approaches by allowing students to actively build their own understanding through hands-on experiences, collaborative problem-solving and scaffolded enquiry, connecting new learning to their prior knowledge and real-world contexts;

- incorporate connectivist approaches to equip students with the digital literacy, critical thinking and networking skills necessary to navigate, evaluate and apply knowledge from the vast and dynamic information landscape of the 21st century, leveraging AI for personalised learning and interdisciplinary connections.

By *combining* the learning sciences, curriculum designers can create dynamic, structured and forward-thinking educational experiences that prepare students not just for examinations, but for lifelong learning in a complex, digital world.

CRITICISM OF CURRICULUM DESIGN AND SEQUENCING

Biesta (2009) highlights a critical concern regarding the dominant focus on 'learning' within contemporary education. He contends that discussions about education have become almost exclusively centred on what can be measured, leading to a situation where we risk 'valuing what we measure' rather than 'measuring what we value' (2009: 33). Furthermore, he argues that the 'learnification' (2009: 36) of education – that is, the pervasive shift in educational vocabulary and practice towards concepts of 'learning' and 'students' – has inadvertently contributed to the disappearance of explicit discussions about educational purpose.

Biesta argues that this learnification is partly an outcome of several trends, including 'the rise of new theories of learning that have put emphasis on the active role of students in the construction of knowledge and understanding and the more facilitating role of teachers in this' (2009: 38). While not explicitly naming learning sciences, these 'new theories of learning' align with key tenets often explored within the field of learning sciences which focus on individual cognitive processes and student-centred approaches to knowledge acquisition.

Therefore, Biesta's argument, when referencing the implications of a focus akin to that in the learning sciences, suggests that while understanding how students learn and the role of learning sciences is valuable, an over-reliance on the language of learning risks obscuring the fundamental 'why' and 'what for' of education. He advocates for reconnecting with the question of purpose through his framework of qualification, socialisation and subjectification, arguing that these dimensions collectively address what constitutes 'good education' beyond merely effective learning processes. This approach aims to reintroduce explicit engagement with values and aims that learnification tends to overlook, ensuring that decisions about education are informed by what we truly value, rather than merely what is easily measurable through learning outcomes.

Biesta argues that to reconnect with the crucial question of educational purpose and to determine what constitutes 'good education' (2009: 41), it is necessary to systematically distinguish between three fundamental functions of education: qualification, socialisation and subjectification. These functions are presented as a composite framework for discussing the aims and ends of education, acknowledging that they are interrelated but require distinct rationales.

QUALIFICATION

This function directly addresses the knowledge, skills, understanding, dispositions and forms of judgement that a subject curriculum aims to impart, enabling students to 'do something'. It prompts curriculum designers to clearly define the specific competencies students should acquire, from vocational skills to political or cultural literacy, and to sequence content in a logical progression that builds these capabilities. For example, in mathematics, this involves outlining the sequence for acquiring mathematical knowledge, skills and understanding to become proficient.

While often linked to economic arguments and workforce preparation, Biesta reminds us that qualification also includes broader literacies essential for functioning in society, such as political or cultural literacy. Curriculum designers must consider the full breadth of these qualifying aims.

SOCIALISATION

This function highlights how the curriculum, both explicitly and implicitly, shapes students into members of particular social, cultural and political 'orders'. Every subject carries messages about importance, values and traditions. As a result, curriculum designers must consider the norms and values embedded in the chosen content and pedagogy, and ask questions such as, how does the curriculum transmit cultural traditions, professional ethics, or societal expectations? For instance, including mathematics in the curriculum and giving it prominence in testing conveys a message about its importance, thereby socialising students into a world where mathematics is valued.

Biesta's argument encourages an awareness of the 'hidden curriculum' (2009: 40), recognising that even if socialisation isn't an explicit aim, it will still occur through the very structure and presentation of a subject. This prompts curriculum designers to be intentional about the social messages their subject conveys.

SUBJECTIFICATION

This function focuses on fostering individuation and independence from existing orders, helping students become autonomous, critical and unique subjects rather than mere reproductions of predefined templates. This is often seen as the opposite of socialisation. A curriculum aiming for subjectification would sequence learning opportunities that promote critical thinking, independent exploration and the ability to respond responsibly to difference. It encourages moving beyond rote learning to foster deeper understanding and personal agency. For example, in mathematics, this could involve exploring how mathematical reasoning can help students form a more autonomous position towards tradition or common sense or even exploring the moral possibilities of mathematics (e.g., division in relation to sharing or justice).

Biesta's arguments prompt curriculum designers to ask whether education is genuinely contributing to students becoming more autonomous and independent in their thinking and acting, rather than just equipping them to fit into existing structures. He stresses that these three functions are interrelated and overlapping, not entirely separate. Curriculum design and sequencing should acknowledge that engaging in qualification will also impact socialisation and subjectification, and vice versa. While synergy is possible, there can also be potential for conflict, particularly between qualification/ socialisation and subjectification.

Biesta provides practical examples in secondary school subjects to illustrate these points clearly:

- *citizenship education*: curriculum discussions can move beyond just providing knowledge (qualification) or aiming for a predefined 'responsible citizen' (socialisation). Instead, they can ask how the curriculum can contribute to political subjectification, fostering political agency that goes beyond reproducing existing templates, allowing students to critically analyse political processes and practices and take initiative. This impacts the choice of topics, teaching methods (e.g., debate, project-based learning) and assessment criteria (2009: 42);

- *mathematics education*: beyond developing mathematical proficiency (qualification), the curriculum could be designed to socialise students into the value and practices of 'mathematising'. More profoundly, it can foster subjectification by encouraging students to use mathematical reasoning to develop an autonomous or considered stance towards tradition, or to explore moral dimensions through mathematical concepts. This would influence the types of problems presented, the emphasis on proof and critical thinking and connections to real-world ethical dilemmas (2009: 43).

In summary, Biesta's framework compels curriculum designers and those involved in sequencing secondary school subjects to engage in explicit, value-based discussions about the aims and ends of education. By consciously addressing how a subject contributes to qualification, socialisation and subjectification, they can create curricula that are not merely effective, but genuinely 'good', fostering a more holistic and purposeful educational experience.

CONCLUSION

As you begin to design and deliver sequences of learning, it is important that you reflect on how your subject curriculum reflects a balance between qualification (skills and knowledge), socialisation (values and norms) and subjectification (student autonomy and agency).

PRACTICAL APPLICATION

The UK government *Reducing Teacher Workload Policy* (2018) states clearly that pre-service teachers should be provided with already existing lesson plans and sequences of learning to help them to reduce the burden of lesson planning, which new teachers report takes an excessively long time. However, it is important that when these existent plans are supplied, inexperienced teachers should be able to understand the learning sciences behind the planning and feel empowered to adapt them if they do not feel they are suitable for the students in front of them. As such, teachers should scrutinise the lesson plans through the lens of learning sciences, and question how or why the learning sciences have been utilised to support the learning, as well as whether there might be a better way of sequencing the individual lesson or sequence of learning for those students.

CONSIDER THIS: THE WIDER CURRICULUM OFFER

Thinking about the school's curriculum and wider offer:

- what does the school's curriculum reveal about the priorities of the school and which subjects are valued most?

- is the content included in the curriculum because it's measurable, or because it's meaningful?

- how can you best align your teaching not only with best practice, but also with the deeper purpose of education?

Below is an example of a single lesson plan that spells out the aspects of each learning science used within it. This demonstrates our argument that all the learning sciences are valuable within lessons and provides an example of the sorts of things you should be looking for when you are presented with lesson plans, before you teach them. You can see how the lesson is sequenced to support students to achieve the learning objectives.

LESSON PLAN: CREATING THE CHARACTER OF AN ELDERLY PERSON

Year Group: Year 7 (mixed ability)

Subject: Drama

Topic: Characterisation – physicality and voice of an elderly person

Duration: 60 minutes

LEARNING OBJECTIVES

By the end of this lesson, students will be able to:

- identify and articulate key physical and vocal characteristics associated with elderly people [cognitivism];

- explore and embody various physical postures, gaits and vocal qualities to portray an elderly character [constructivism];

- collaborate effectively with peers to develop and refine character ideas [constructivism, behaviourism];

- utilise online resources to research and critically evaluate representations of elderly people [connectivism];

- reflect on their own learning process and provide constructive feedback to peers [cognitivism, constructivism].

MATERIALS

- Whiteboard/projector.

- Pictures/short video clips of diverse elderly people (real-life, not caricatures) [connectivism, cognitivism].

- Access to internet-enabled devices (e.g., tablets, laptops) for research [connectivism].

- Worksheet with prompts for observation and reflection [cognitivism, constructivism].

- Space for movement and improvisation.

- Reward system (e.g., house points, merits) [behaviourism].

LEARNING SCIENCES FOCUS

This lesson will blend:

- *behaviourism*: through clear routines, consistent expectations and positive reinforcement to manage the learning environment and encourage participation;

- *cognitivism*: by activating prior knowledge, managing cognitive load, building mental schemas for characterisation and facilitating metacognitive reflection;

- *constructivism*: by encouraging active learning, collaborative exploration and real-world contextualisation of character development, allowing students to build their own understanding through experience and interaction;

- *connectivism*: by engaging students in networked learning, utilising diverse online resources and fostering critical evaluation of information to inform their character choices.

LESSON ACTIVITIES

1. **Prompt start and 'do now' (5 minutes)**

   - *routine*: as students enter the classroom, the teacher stands at the door, greeting them warmly and setting immediate expectations for entering the learning space;

   - *do now task*: students immediately sit down and complete a short-written task: 'List three physical traits and three vocal qualities you associate with an elderly person' [cognitivism: activating prior knowledge/schema theory; behaviourism: clear routine and expectation for prompt start];

   - *behaviourism in action*: the teacher uses precise praise for students who settle quickly and begin the task without prompting (e.g., 'Thank you, [student name], for getting straight to work and showing excellent focus').

2. **Introduction: what makes a character 'elderly'? (10 minutes)**

   - *cognitivism*: briefly review some of the do now responses, prompting students to share initial ideas, thereby activating their existing schemas about elderly people;

   - *connectivism and dual coding*: display a range of diverse images and short, respectful video clips (20–30 seconds each) of elderly people in various real-life situations (e.g., walking, talking, doing hobbies). Discuss different physicalities and vocal tones observed;

   - *teacher guidance*: emphasise that we are observing for authentic characteristics, not stereotypes. Prompt students to consider: 'What physical changes might happen to a person as they age? How might their voice change?'

   - *cognitive load management*: keep the video clips very short and focused to avoid overwhelming working memory;

   - *discussion*: facilitate a brief discussion on the observed differences, challenging any immediate stereotypical assumptions. 'Are all elderly people the same?'

3. **Collaborative exploration and research (15 minutes)**

   - *constructivism and connectivism*: divide students into small groups (three to four). Each group will be given a specific aspect to research or focus on (e.g., posture and gait, hand gestures and facial expressions, vocal tone and pace of speech);

   - *task:*

     o *online research*: using provided devices, groups will research examples of their assigned aspect related to elderly people. Provide a curated list of reliable educational websites or video platforms (e.g., documentaries, interviews with elderly individuals, not comedic sketches) to guide their search

     o *critical evaluation*: guide students to critically evaluate their sources. 'Is this a respectful portrayal? Does it seem authentic? Who created this content and why?'

- o *physical/vocal exploration*: groups then physically and vocally explore and experiment with their findings. One student might try different postures while others observe and provide feedback

- o *scaffolding and ZPD*: the teacher circulates, offering targeted support and prompts – for example, 'Can you try making that movement smaller? How does a slower pace affect the sound of your voice?' This support helps students achieve tasks they cannot accomplish alone, pushing them through their ZPD

- o *behaviourism*: use group praise for effective collaboration and focused exploration ('Excellent teamwork in Group 3, I see everyone contributing and experimenting');

4. **Character development in pairs (15 minutes)**

- *constructivism*: students work in pairs to develop a short, non-verbal improvisation (e.g., an elderly person trying to pick something up, crossing the road, or reacting to a surprise);

- *task:*

  - o *apply learning*: students apply their observations and group explorations to create a character. Encourage them to consider their chosen physical and vocal characteristics

  - o *peer feedback*: after a minute of improvisation, pairs switch roles. Then, they provide constructive feedback to each other using specific prompts from the worksheet (e.g., 'I noticed you used [physical trait]; how did this affect your character's age? What was most effective? What could be further developed?')

  - o *cognitivism* (*metacognition*): the worksheet prompts encourage self-evaluation and reflection on their choices and their partner's performance

  - o *scaffolding*: the worksheet provides sentence starters for feedback, acting as a temporary support for students to articulate their observations effectively;

5. **Showcase and reflection (10 minutes)**

- *constructivism*: invite a few volunteer pairs to share their short improvisations with the class;

- *whole-class feedback*: after each performance, facilitate a brief class discussion:

  - o *teacher as facilitator*: 'What did you observe? What was effective in conveying age?'

  - o *connectivism*: connect back to the diversity of representations discussed earlier. 'Did this portrayal feel authentic or stereotypical? Why?';

- *cognitivism* (*metacognition and retrieval practice*): ask students to individually complete an exit ticket (low-stakes recall): 'Name one physical or vocal technique you learned today to portray an elderly character, and one thing you found challenging.' This serves as retrieval practice and encourages metacognitive reflection on their learning;

- *behaviourism*: end the lesson with a clear signal for attention and a positive closing, perhaps praising the overall effort and engagement of the class.

6. **Adaptations**

- *support:*

  - o pre-assign roles/tasks within groups for collaborative activities o   provide specific example phrases for vocal exploration (e.g., 'a tired sigh', 'a slow, deliberate sentence')

o   model physical prompts (e.g., 'try slouching', 'try shuffling your feet')

o   pair less confident students with more experienced ones for character development

o   more explicit scaffolding during online research (e.g., direct links rather than general search terms);

• *challenge:*

o   encourage more able students to combine multiple physical and vocal traits simultaneously

o   ask them to justify their character choices in detail, linking back to their research

o   challenge them to think about the emotional state that might accompany their chosen physicality and voice

o   ask them to critically compare their created character with examples found online, explaining similarities and differences.

7. **Assessment**

• *formative assessment:*

o   teacher observation of group collaboration, exploration and application of techniques

o   quality of peer feedback and self-reflection on worksheets/exit tickets

o   participation in class discussions

o   engagement with online resources and critical evaluation skills;

• *behaviourism*: positive reinforcement for engagement and effort throughout the lesson.

CHAPTER SUMMARY

This chapter explored how the learning sciences informed curriculum design and sequencing in secondary education. It began by defining curriculum design as the intentional planning of what pupils learned, when they learned it and how learning built over time. Sequencing, meanwhile, referred to the logical organisation of content to support cumulative understanding and retention. The chapter then examined how each learning science contributed to curriculum design. A detailed drama lesson plan illustrated how these theories could be blended in practice, showing how learning objectives, activities and assessments could be aligned with multiple theoretical principles. The chapter also engaged with Biesta's critique of the learnification of education, which prioritised measurable outcomes over educational purpose. His framework, qualification, socialisation and subjectification offered a way to reconnect with the broader aims of education, encouraging curriculum designers to consider not only what pupils learned, but why they learned it and who they became through the process. Ultimately, the chapter advocated for a thoughtful, blended approach to curriculum design and sequencing, one that was responsive to learners' needs, grounded in theory and mindful of the values and purposes that underpinned education.

REFLECTIVE QUESTIONS: CHAPTER 9

Think about a recent lesson or unit you taught or observed.

- Which learning sciences were most evident in its design?
- Were there opportunities for retrieval practice, collaborative learning, or digital exploration?
- What challenges do you face in adapting curriculum sequencing for different students?

——— FURTHER READING ————————————————————

ITTECF 3.1 A school's curriculum enables it to set out its vision for the knowledge, skills and values that its pupils will learn, encompassing the national curriculum within a coherent wider vision for successful learning.

Rosenshine, B. (2012). Principles of instruction: research-based strategies that all teachers should know. *American Educator*, 36(1), 12–20.

Rosenshine's *principles of instruction* are rooted in cognitive science and provide practical guidance for sequencing, such as reviewing prior learning, presenting new material in small steps and checking for understanding. This widely cited paper underpins much of the ITTECF guidance on curriculum and pedagogy. It outlines ten research-based principles that support effective teaching which are directly linked to curriculum sequencing, as they emphasise the importance of building knowledge incrementally and revisiting key concepts to strengthen long-term memory.

——— REFERENCES ————————————————————

Biesta, G. (2009). Good education in an age of measurement: on the need to reconnect with the question of purpose in education. *Educational Assessment, Evaluation and Accountability*, 21(1), 33–46. https://doi.org/10.1007/s11092-008-9064-9

Bruner, J. S. (1966). *Towards a Theory of Instruction*. New York: W. W. Norton.

Department for Education (DfE) (2018). *Addressing Teacher Workload in Initial Teacher Education (ITE)*. Available at: https://assets.publishing.service.gov.uk/media/5f57a927d3bf7f723f8f5655/Addressing_Workload_in_ITE.pdf. Accessed 20 November 2025.

Dunlosky, J., Rawson, K. A., Marsh, E. J., Nathan, M. J. and Willingham, D. T. (2013). Improving students' learning with effective learning techniques: promising directions from cognitive and educational psychology. *Psychological Science in the Public Interest*, 14(1), 4–58. https://doi.org/10.1177/1529100612453266

Kagan, S. (1994). *Cooperative Learning*. San Clemente, CA: Kagan.

Rosenshine, B. (2012). Principles of instruction: Research-based strategies that all teachers should know. *American Educator*, 36(1), 12–20.

Unwin, A. and Yandell, J. (2017). *Rethinking Education: Whose Knowledge is it Anyway?* Oxford: New Internationalist.

Vygotsky, L. S. (1978). *Mind in Society: The Development of Higher Psychological Processes.* Cambridge, MA: Harvard University Press.

10

ADAPTATIONS OF PLANNING TO DIVERSE LEARNER NEEDS

LEARNING OUTCOMES

By reading this chapter you will develop:

- **An understanding of why adaptations of planning may be required to meet the diverse needs of learners**
- **Confidence in using some of the approaches to incorporating different learning theories while supporting learners with diverse needs**
- **An understanding of some of the complexities of using different learning theories while supporting learning with diverse needs**

INITIAL TEACHER TRAINING AND EARLY CAREER FRAMEWORK (ITTECF)

The key reading from the ITTECF that is to be explored within this chapter is:

Davis, P., Florian, L., Ainscow, M., Dyson, A., Farrell, P., Hick, P. and Rouse, M. (2004). *Teaching Strategies and Approaches for Pupils with Special Educational Needs: A Scoping Study* (Research Report No. 516). DfES. https://dera.ioe.ac.uk/6059/1/RR516.pdf

INTRODUCTION

This chapter addresses the fundamental necessity for teachers to adapt their planning and pedagogical approaches to cater to the varied needs of every student. It provides an understanding of why such adaptations are required and aims to build confidence in using different learning theories to support learners with diverse needs, while also exploring the complexities inherent in this process. The chapter emphasises that effective adaptation begins with thoroughly understanding individual students, including their interests, motivations, responses to strategies and their perceived abilities within subjects. It explores key areas of diverse needs, such as special educational needs and disabilities (SEND), varying levels of prior attainment, differences in cultural capital and the specific challenges faced by English as an additional language (EAL) learners. By drawing on research-informed strategies from various learning theories, including behaviourism, constructivism and cognitivism, this chapter provides a framework for effective, inclusive and adaptive planning

ADAPTING FOR YOUR STUDENTS

As we move through this chapter, it is important to start by noting that the best and most effective method for supporting you in adapting to your students' diverse needs is, first and foremost, to get to know your individual students. Identify what interests and motivates them, which strategies they respond to effectively or not, as well as their ability and perceived ability within their given subject. The use of pupil profiles and/or educational healthcare plans (EHCPs), where available, will aid you in this, as well as reviewing previous progress data alongside discussions with experienced colleagues. It is also important to understand that *diverse learner needs* is a wide and varied topic; this chapter cannot encompass it in its entirety and therefore is designed to highlight some key common themes and strategies you may come across. It aims to provide research-informed information around how learning theories may be used to support effective adaptive planning for some more common diverse needs as a launch pad for your own reflections and further independent research on areas that are most relevant to you and your school setting.

SPECIAL EDUCATIONAL NEEDS AND DISABILITIES (SEND) CODE OF PRACTICE: FOUR AREAS OF NEED

The DfE's SEND code of practice (2015) outlines four areas of need to help support students with special educational needs and disabilities (SEND). These areas include:

- *communication and interaction*, which covers difficulties with speech, language and social communication;

- *cognition and learning*, which covers a broad range of learning difficulties including dyslexia, dyscalculia and dyspraxia, ranging from mild to profound in severity;

- *social, emotional and mental health* (SEMH), which covers a variety of needs including anxiety, depression and a variety of behaviour difficulties, such as those associated with attention deficit hyperactive disorder (ADHD) and autism;

- *sensory and/or physical needs*, which may include visual or hearing impairment and physical difficulties.

At this point it is important to note that, though divided into these four categories, a lot of complex SEND, such as ADHD and autism will fall in to multiple categories and the way they are expressed both in and out of the classroom with vary from individual to individual – again, this is why it is so important to work on an individual basis with each child to identify the strategies that best suit that student's needs.

For many of these areas of needs the use of behaviourism strategies such as *applied behavioural analysis* (ABA) – which uses the key principles of *discrete trail training* (DTT), where skills are broken down into small, manageable steps that are taught systematically – and *consistent positive reinforcement* are used to reinforce and encourage positive behaviour while also working to reduce the behaviours that interfere with learning and social interactions. Leaf et al. (2016), found this an effective strategy for improving communication skills in students with autism as it provides structures and protocols which can be followed by the student and teacher, while also remaining flexible for in-the-moment adjustments based on individual needs. In addition to this, it has been noted that the use of *behaviour contracts* and *structured environments* also helps support students with SEMH. As a study by Halliwell (2025) found, creating an environment that celebrates strengths and encouraging students to take risks, in a perceived safe environment, helps build a positive self-perception for the student and, by recognising small successes, helps improve their self-esteem.

When considering constructivism, peer, collaborative or social learning and the zone of proximal development (ZPD) are often identified as effective strategies for developing children with SEND. Bada (2015) and Zajda (2021) have both highlighted that a constructivist classroom improves critical thinking and problem-solving skills, and enhances cognitive development by allowing instructions to be tailored to individuals; they discuss the need for students to be actively engaged in the learning process through cognitive, emotional and social interactions to allow them to engage in knowledge construction. Explicit instruction could be quite inflexible depending on the type and severity of SEND in the classroom and the specific task or topic. In turn, offering opportunities to develop social and communication skills with their peers in a structured and supportive environment can ensure any underdeveloped skills, due to SEND, are enhanced and future outcomes optimised. Furthermore, by allowing students to work within the ZPD with appropriate scaffolding (Wood et al., 1976), all students can operate at a level that is achievable with support, but is just beyond their current ability, which is instrumental in building their self-confidence.

Additionally, peer-assisted learning within the ZPD not only reinforces the concepts being taught by enabling collaboration with more knowledgeable peers, but it also helps to develop social and communication skills. For students with sensory and/or physical needs, this approach provides valuable support through their peers, as well as through technology-assisted learning tools, adaptive tools, or visual aids, allowing them to engage in activities in a way that is accessible to them and promotes their active participation.

Cognitive strategies can also play a crucial role in supporting students with SEND. By using metacognitive strategies, students are encouraged to self-monitor and reflect on their skills and learning progress; from this, they can use goal-setting techniques to create steps for future improvement. The Education Endowment Foundation's (EEF's) guidance report (EEF, 2021) supports this by stating that research highlights the importance of explicitly teaching metacognitive strategies in lessons, particularly to SEND students who benefit from structured self-monitoring and cognitive scaffolding. However, it notes that to do this effectively, it must be paired with explicit instruction and scaffolding to support all students in understanding how to approach each task.

In addition, it is important to be aware that all students have different capacities when it comes to working memory and cognitive load, and these limitations may make it harder for students with SEND to recall and organise knowledge (Gear, 2022). Therefore, using techniques that reduce the cognitive load on the working memory, such as dual coding, sentence starters, graphic organisers and task chunking, can be effective strategies for supporting students with lower working memory capacities. Furthermore, regular structured retrieval practice can enhance memory recall and reduce cognitive overload, as it helps students store, retrieve and apply information more effectively. It has been noted that when the retrieval of this information is more active, such as in self-testing activities (Karpicke and Blunt, 2011), this improves retention more effectively than passive review.

Lastly, a key aspect of the ITTECF that recommends teachers used worked examples can be counterproductive if you are teaching students with reduced working memory. This is because they cannot hold sufficient steps in their working memory during the worked example explanation. You should refrain from using worked examples with students who have underdeveloped or lesser working memory.

LOWER AND HIGHER PRIOR-ATTAINING STUDENTS

Prior attainment is the baseline used by the DfE when calculating a student's Key Stage 4 progress 8 and attainment 8 scores, the expected progress and attainment a student will achieve across eight qualifications in a state secondary school from the end of primary school to the end of Key Stage 4, using Key Stage 2 scaled scores in English reading and maths (DfE, 2025). Those with an averaged scaled score of below 100 are identified as low prior attainers (LPAs). Equal to or above 110 are identified as higher prior attainers (HPAs) and anyone in between these two scores is identified as a middle prior attainer (MPA). This provides a starting point for teachers to indicate a student's current academic abilities as they begin their secondary education. It is important to note, however, that these abilities can be influenced by many non-academic factors throughout a student's school life, including their personal background and life experiences, as well as their attitude towards school and learning, behaviour and mental health. These factors may have a short- or long-term impact on their level of progress and attainment at any point during their academic career. Therefore, as stated at the beginning of this chapter, it is beneficial for teachers to get to know their individual students beyond their LPA, MPA, or HPA labels and to endeavour to understand how to best support everyone in the classroom.

Despite the complexity around identifying LPA and HPA students, it can still be considered beneficial to plan and adapt learning to meet the needs of students who would fall into these categories. Often, teachers can be found to 'teach to the middle' in an aim to capture as many students as possible.

Frequently, this results in LPA students missing the vital support and scaffolding required to allow them to access the work, while at the same HPA students become bored and disengaged as they find the work too easy and not challenging enough, both of which can lead to disruption in learning. This directly relates to the concept of cognitive load theory and is often referred to as *desirable difficulty*. Work needs to be of an optimal difficulty for strong memories to be formed. Too easy or too hard and strong memories are not formed effectively. Therefore, your knowledge of learning theories can become a powerful tool in tackling both ends of the spectrum of learners.

Your first consideration should be the cognitive ability of LPA and HPA students during any particular subject, task or topic; how this might differ; and the cognitive load this might put on their working memory. Generally speaking, HPA students will have a higher cognitive ability for the sorts of tasks that are used to measure students (which is why we often refer to them as higher *attainers* rather than higher *ability*) and therefore can be challenged by encouraging the use of reflective metacognitive practices to allow them to better understand how they learn and can use this to self-motivate themselves to push themselves to produce higher-quality work (Flavell, 1979). They should be able to also deal with and process more complex and extensive sets of instructions and more abstract concepts. LPA students (who will have been less successful in the unscaffolded or unsupported tasks found in formal assessments) may need instructions broken down into more digestible chunks with dual coding or visual support to aid this (Jones, 2025). They may also benefit from more explicit teaching strategies, where they are shown techniques and processes for organising information more effectively, reducing the cognitive and metacognitive loads respectively.

It is important, therefore, to consider Vygotsky's ZPD (Vygotsky, 1978) and ensure that all students are working in an area of suitable challenge with appropriate levels of support. For a student with HPA, this might involve a strong focus on enquiry or problem-based learning, where they must explore concepts and apply knowledge to generate solutions. Conversely, with LPA students, this might involve providing additional scaffolding and support tools, such as sentence starters, to help them complete a task.

Furthermore, the constructivism strategy of peer collaboration can provide powerful support for both LPA and HPA students simultaneously. It fosters a shared learning experience and promotes inclusivity, as higher attainers can act as what Vygotsky calls 'more capable peers', reinforcing their own understanding by explaining concepts and developing their analytical skills by modelling and explaining their reasoning. In turn, lower attainers gain access to more advanced thinking processes through guided interactions and can improve their understanding and address misconceptions through structured dialogue with peers. This may also result in increased confidence and motivation if these interactions are positive (EEF, 2025).

Finally, behaviourism, through positive reinforcement, can be used to reward progress and encourage self-directed learning regardless of prior attainment. This is particularly effective if the focus is on reinforcing progress rather than just the final outcome, as students with lower prior attainment can quickly become disheartened if rewards are based solely on comparing themselves to their higher-attaining peers.

It is crucial to consider and present positive reinforcement in a consistent and fair manner across all students to ensure equal opportunities and avoid double standards. Pairing this with personalised feedback that provides targeted guidance is also important, as this allows each individual student to make progress suitable to their ability. Hattie and Timperley (2007) discuss the merit of constructive feedback, noting that it can challenge the thinking of students with higher prior attainment and encourage deeper analysis, while, in turn, providing clear, actionable feedback that guides students with lower prior attainment without overwhelming them. While each type of feedback may look significantly different and require students to act on it in different ways, they both offer opportunities for a student to progress at a level suitable to their current ability.

LIVED EXPERIENCES AND CULTURAL CAPITAL

As alluded to above, students' backgrounds and lived experiences can have a significant impact on their progress, attainment, attitudes, behaviour in the classroom and their overall mental health; therefore, it is important to consider and adapt to these factors when planning and delivering lessons. In addition, a student's cultural capital, which can be considered as the social assets that contribute to a person's ability to succeed in society (Bourdieu, 1986), can also affect their ability to learn.

For example, students with higher cultural capital often (but not always) have greater exposure to books, discussions and experiences that support and enrich their understanding, and increase their familiarity with academic language, allowing them to more easily engage with learning materials. This also provides confidence in engaging in social and academic situations and allows them to understand and more easily meet the cultural norms and expectations of a school environment compared to their peers with lower cultural capital. This often links heavily with students from lower socio-economic backgrounds who frequently have less access to books, technology and enrichment activities compared to their peers from higher socio-economic backgrounds (DfE (Australia), 2025). In turn, this can limit their ability to engage in cultural capital experiences and learning in general. This can also result in negative effects on their mental health and well-being, leading to lower motivation and engagement, which, when paired with the trend of higher school absence rates for disadvantaged students, can widen the attainment gap between them and their peers, exacerbating the impact on their well-being and mental health and creating a dangerous cycle.

It has been considered that the explicit teaching of metacognitive and self-regulatory strategies is often beneficial in supporting students from disadvantaged backgrounds as it encourages them to actively engage with learning materials by asking themselves questions such as, 'What do I already know?' or 'How can I approach this problem?' This allows them to consider how they can best approach a task. Planning, goal-setting and monitoring progress also enable students to break tasks down into manageable steps, track their improvements and develop independence. This is important as it helps students regulate their own learning process, which is particularly beneficial for those who struggle with independent study, a common issue for students from a disadvantaged background (Zimmerman, 2002).

Furthermore, a collaborative learning approach, as suggested by constructivism, offers several benefits to learners from disadvantaged backgrounds. Mainly, it provides shared accountability which encourages engagement and makes students feel valued, while also supporting the student through peer discussions, tutoring and collaborative problem-solving. This, in turn, reduces the potential pressure to succeed on the individual and can prevent disengagement (EEF, 2025). However, it also has the dual benefit of peer modelling, where students can interact with, observe and imitate peers from a diverse range of backgrounds and lived experiences in how they engage with and approach the academic, social and cultural norms of the school environment.

ENGLISH AS AN ADDITIONAL LANGUAGE (EAL)

Students who are identified as English as an additional language (EAL) learners can vary greatly in their ability to understand and communicate effectively in English. However, regardless of their proficiency, this often impacts their ability to learn, influencing their cognitive development, academic achievement and social integration. EAL students typically experience a higher cognitive load as they must process both subject content and language simultaneously, with more limited proficiency making it harder to engage with complex academic materials (The Bell Foundation, 2025).

This, in turn, can cause EAL students to struggle with attainment, particularly in subjects that require strong literacy skills. Consequently, these barriers may also impact their confidence and willingness to participate and, in some extreme cases, can lead to social isolation from peers as they struggle to communicate effectively with them. However, a long-term study by Lindorff et al. (2025) suggests that EAL students can outperform native English speakers once they achieve language proficiency.

When thinking about strategies to support EAL learners, scaffolding techniques lay the foundation. Temporary supports such as visual aids, sentence starters, modelling language use and guided reading all help EAL learners engage with complex materials as they develop their language skills and ensure extraneous cognitive load is reduced. These can be removed over time, as they become more competent and independent, to maintain the desirable difficulty. This should be paired with explicit vocabulary instruction and the direct teaching of essential vocabulary through a contextualised approach and semantic mapping, which connects words with meanings and examples, such as in the use of the Frayer model (Frayer et al., 1969), to help EAL students understand subject-specific terminology and general academic language. In addition, peer-assisted learning, where the EAL learner is paired with a fluent peer, reinforces language skills, allowing them to observe, imitate and practise English in an authentic, low-pressure environment.

Additionally, the consideration of behaviourist approaches is important. As with all learners, positive reinforcement, correction and encouragement can help reinforce correct language use. Paired with clear instructions and predictable routines, broken down into small, manageable steps, this reduces cognitive load while providing a predictable and secure environment to engage within (The Bell Foundation, 2018). Activities such as drills and repetitions, choral reading and word-matching tasks allow them to practise key vocabulary and sentence structures to strengthen retention. However, it is important to note that while these may help with the memorisation of specific spellings and sentence structures, they do not always provide a deeper or contextualised understanding.

CONCLUSION

When adapting to meet the diverse needs of learners, it is important to consider the different learning theories together in unity with each other rather than as separate strategies and approaches, carefully selecting the concepts, techniques or approaches in each theory that will blend most effectivity to ensure the success of the activity or task set, while also best supporting the needs of the learners who must complete it.

CONSIDER THIS: BEST PRACTICE

Consider what you feel is best practice in supporting students with SEND.

- Do you have an anecdote or example of where you have seen effective use of a learning theory's technique to support specific learners' needs?

- Do you have an anecdote or example of where you have seen an ineffective use of a learning theory's techniques to support specific learners' needs?

PRACTICAL APPLICATION

Behaviourism, cognitivism, constructivism and connectivism all have clear benefits for supporting a wide range of diverse learner needs, in a variety of ways. Therefore, it is important to consider what some of these might look like in practice and how they might be embedded into planning and delivery.

CONSIDER THIS: DIVERSE NEEDS

Consider the diverse needs of the learners in a classroom environment you have experienced. In reflecting on this, think about:

- how effective behaviourism strategies can ensure a safe and consistent environment for all learners;

- how effective and carefully planned constructivist activities can help develop the social and communication skills of all learners;

- the cognitive and metacognitive strategies that could most easily and effectively be implemented to support the widest range of learners with diverse needs;

- how you might interweave key concepts from each learning theory to create a highly effective activity that can support most of the learners' needs effectively, and what limitations and additional requirements this might create to allow all to be successful.

PLANNING FOR LEARNERS WITH SEND

Learners with social, emotional and mental health issues or cognition and learning challenges commonly struggle with organisation, time management and even just knowing where to start on a task. Therefore, providing a list of tasks for them to work through provides structure, helps them to process and organise themselves and gives them a clear starting point, which, in turn, may reduce anxiety or procrastination. This can most commonly be seen in a science practical lesson, where a student is given a clear, step-by-step list to follow to work logically through the experiment from start to completion. However, this strategy could be easily utilised in other lessons, such as providing a series of steps a student needs to follow to complete a maths equation, the structure of or points to include in a history or English essay, or even just a step-by-step lesson journey so they know each activity they will encounter and can keep track as they move through the lesson.

Pairing this with a specific visual timer will also help keep them on track and engaged as they will know how much time they have to complete each task. However, careful consideration of the amount of time given must be taken, as too little time could lead to anxiety that they might not complete the task, while too much time may lead to them becoming bored, disengaged, or distracted. This will depend on each student individually and will become easier as you get to know their abilities and levels of motivation.

For those with communication and language barriers, the priority is to consider how you can best remove those barriers to allow them to access the learning. Key word lists and sentence starters are good scaffolding tools for those who have difficulties in written communication, such as those with dyslexia, as they provide starting points for them to build their written work from. The use of low-stakes spelling quizzes may also help them develop their understanding of the spelling of key written words as they get to practise and rehearse the spellings. However, it is important to note that these do not always support the use of those words in context and may cause levels of anxiety that you need to be aware of.

In terms of verbal communication, opportunities to think–pair–share before a class discussion allow students time to prepare their answers and responses and work on how they can verbally communicate their ideas before being called on. In this approach, students can process their thoughts individually, then organise and rehearse communicating them with a peer before sharing with the rest of the class. This could also be done individually by posing a question, pausing, calling a name and then repeating the question; this gives students time to think and organise a response before they are called on. Choral and group reading of texts, in English and drama, for example, will also allow them to verbally participate in a low-stakes environment. *Popcorn reading*, where a student reads aloud a minimum of one sentence or as much as they like before passing on to another student, is a popular method as it gives the student control over how much they participate while still expecting them to do so.

As set out in the various chapters, collaborative strategies such as think–pair–share, peer and collaborative learning all help support a wide range of students with SEND. Collaborative problem-solving in mathematics, where groups or pairs work together to solve complex problems, has been seen to encourage participation, reduce anxiety and strengthen problem-solving skills. Reciprocal reading in English, where pairs take it in turn to read a passage aloud and summarise key points, has been seen to improve reading fluency, comprehension and verbal expression. Peer feedback in creative subjects such as art and drama helps students build confidence and social skills through collaborative creativity, especially when paired with giving them a specific role to focus on, such as director or stage manager in drama, or recording observations or explaining results in science.

PLANNING FOR HIGHER AND LOWER PRIOR-ATTAINING STUDENTS

When planning for students with higher and lower prior attainment, it is important to think carefully about cognitive load and what is achievable for them, and how you will allow them to work in the appropriate ZPD. This may differ for each student in the class.

Targeted questioning is likely the simplest and most effective way to ensure this occurs in your lesson. Considering the challenge or cognitive load of the question you are posing can quickly allow you to adapt the challenge to the needs of the students. Using tools like Bloom's taxonomy (Bloom, 1956), which suggests that 'state' or 'describe' questions have a lower cognitive load than more complex questions such as 'analyse' or 'evaluate', can help you identify the challenge in the question as well as offer strategies to scaffold the question down to support all students in answering it.

For example, if we take the following geography question: 'Analyse the impact of urbanisation on water supply in developing countries', this requires students to break down the causes and effects, consider multiple perspectives such as environmental, economic and social impacts, and link the ideas of how urbanisation can lead to issues with water supply. This creates a high cognitive load as they must apply multiple different skills and concepts. The question could be scaffolded down by asking students to simply 'state what urbanisation is', or 'describe the environmental impacts of urbanisation', or 'explain how urbanisation might cause water pollution'. By breaking up the question, you are providing all the different components that a student could use and piece together to answer the originally posed question, resulting in all students being able to answer the original question, even though the journey they took and the support used to get there might have been different.

Rewards and positive praise are seen as great motivators for students to complete work; however, teachers tend to favour more readily praising or rewarding a student who produces a high-quality piece of work or shows high academic achievement. This can be disheartening for students with lower prior attainment, as their quality of work may never reach that level.

Using praise to reward effort and engagement is also an effective motivator. During class discussions, simple sentences such as, 'Thank you for giving that answer, however, it is not quite right; have you considered this …' is a great way to acknowledge their participation and build their confidence while providing specific feedback to help them improve in a supportive manner. This can be paired with the previously mentioned question-scaffolding techniques to help them reach the correct answer, which you can then additionally praise for its academic merit.

A tiered reward system where students earn points, for example in mathematics, for completing practice problems and progressing from simpler to more complex ones can also encourage and motivate learners of different abilities. Options could include starting students at different levels of challenge so they all progress at similar rates at an appropriate level of challenge, or implementing a tiered point system where quick, low-stakes questions are worth fewer points than more challenging, longer questions. Both approaches can level the playing field as lower attainers can quickly collect points for completing lower-stakes questions, while higher attainers can collect more points from doing more challenging questions, providing a more even distribution of points and rewards across all abilities.

Similarly to supporting learners with SEND, peer collaboration is also a great tool to support learners with different levels of prior attainment. For example, in PE, giving students with higher prior attainment the role of coaching or captaining a team would help them develop their leadership, teamwork and communication skills, while also supporting students with lower prior attainment in developing their fundamental skills and ability to play the sport as they are guided by their peers on how to improve. Similarly, in creative subjects, such as design and technology or art, getting students of different abilities and prior attainment to work together and provide peer feedback and evaluation of each other's work promotes leadership skills and encourages reflection for higher-attaining students and provides scaffolding and improves understanding for lower-attaining students. This is especially helpful as their peers might explain the feedback in a different and potentially more accessible way than a teacher. However, with both strategies, it is crucial that you carefully plan and explain the success criteria and the expectations of everyone in their roles, so you can provide structured guidance to ensure that students work effectively and in a constructive manner.

PLANNING FOR STUDENTS WITH DIFFERENT LIVED EXPERIENCES AND CULTURAL CAPITAL

When planning for students with different lived experiences and cultural capital, it is important to consider how you can provide support to allow all students to access the same learning, resources and materials regardless of their background or experiences.

Starting with a subject such as geography, getting students to consider their local community by studying maps and identifying environmental and social challenges builds geographical awareness about an area they should all be comparatively familiar with. They can then take these ideas and begin to connect and apply their knowledge to real-world issues and communities beyond that of their local area, giving all students a foundational understanding to build from.

Real-world issues and problem-solving are often beneficial to learners from disadvantaged backgrounds as they provide relevance to what they are learning, which can increase motivation; this is often something they lack. Completing maths problems relating to budgets, shopping, or planning a trip are examples of this. Similarly, getting students to design a product to solve a real-world problem relevant to them in art or design and technology, such as a school organiser or pencil case, would be effective.

Conversely, providing tasks that introduce students to new experiences – such as historical events and timelines in history, artists and artwork in art, or authors and literature in English – from different cultures, origins, or perspectives will help students experience and develop their own cultural capital while exploring the viewpoints, thoughts, emotions and experiences of others in a safe and structured environment. Pairing this with tasks where students are allowed to create work based on such perspectives representing personal or historical narratives will additionally encourage creativity, self-expression and cultural awareness. For example, students could produce a poem in English or a piece of artwork in art in the style of the artist or author explored or on a particular theme, or they could write a letter or news report about a specific historical event from the perspective of a person living through it.

Hands-on group work and collaborative learning activities, such as devising performances in drama, team-based strategy games in PE and practical work in science, help learners build social skills, confidence and resilience as they work with peers who can act as role models while also encouraging active engagement. Carrying out similar activities in less active subjects, such as reading circles in English or languages, where students work together in groups to read a text with assigned roles (summariser, questioner, vocabulary finder, etc.) would work in a similar way while also supporting their comprehension.

PLANNING FOR STUDENTS WITH ENGLISH AS AN ADDITIONAL LANGUAGE (EAL)

When planning for EAL students, considering how to best allow them to integrate fully into the lesson and the learning is key. Obviously, this will vary greatly depending on the individual and their prior level of understanding of English. However, considering ways to support how they can access the knowledge and concepts is a good place to start. Using gestures, pictures, manipulatives, or more visual representations can help reinforce understanding beyond that of written text or verbal explanations. Students can use these visual representations and begin to associate them with words or concepts. For example, in science, using a model of the heart to explain its structure and how blood moves through it allows students to see the different structures and create an association between them and the word used to name them.

Beyond this, the development of their language and understanding could be considered the next priority. Using models such as the Frayer model (Frayer et al., 1969) requires students to define a word, list its characteristics and give examples and non-examples, building their schema around the word for them to draw upon. Similarly, the use of dual-language word banks in their home language and English also builds their schema as they can link the English word to one they may already be familiar with and the schema they have associated with that. Pairing these with sentence starters and writing frames supports the development of their grammatical understanding of English by providing structure and guidance to their writing, particularly in subjects where essays or reports are common practice, such as English, history, or science.

Finally, as with all the previously discussed needs, peer collaboration is an effective tool, such as in a think–pair–share task, as it provides EAL learners with the opportunity to reflect on their thoughts individually and then work through their thoughts with a peer and develop their verbal response before sharing. This is especially effective if paired with a student with a strong verbal ability in English as it allows that student to model the conventions for spoken English for their EAL learner to mirror and can help provide structure for further discussions in a low-pressure environment compared to being in front of the whole class or a teacher. However, for all the suggestions for EAL learners, repetition and retrieval are key. Using frequent low-level assessments such as informal quizzes and retrieval practice requires the learners to keep returning to the learned content, strengthening their schema and links between their long-term and working memory, allowing for easier retrieval and supporting gradual language acquisition over time.

CHAPTER SUMMARY

As outlined in the examples of application above, there are various ways and points in a lesson where you could effectively include a variety of learning theory strategies to support a wide range of learners with diverse needs. The applications discussed are only a fraction of the possible strategies, and it is up to you as the teacher to find the strategies that work best for the individuals in your classroom while also ensuring that you are delivering appropriate content to the whole class, not just those with additional needs.

This can be a tricky balancing act between doing what is best for an individual and what is best for the whole class. Therefore, it is important to ensure frequent reflection on the effectiveness and purpose of the strategy and carefully consider the processes and structure you are going to put in place to ensure the strategy meets the needs of both you and the class. Whenever you want to implement a new strategy, it is good professional practice to observe expert practitioners who have already developed effective strategies and techniques to support learners with diverse needs, focusing particular attention on how they weave together learning theories and create an environment that is supportive to all. These observations can be within your own department if the practice is already common, or in another department if it is known that the strategy is more effectively embedded elsewhere. Starting a conversation with colleagues whose role is to more frequently observe practice in your department or across the school, such as heads of subject or departments or teaching and learning leads, will help you identify teachers who excel at a given practice and provide the best observation experiences.

This chapter explored the need for effective planning for diverse learners by adapting teaching strategies to align with students' individual abilities, backgrounds and needs. It highlighted that students present unique challenges and strengths due to factors such as SEND, prior attainment, cultural capital, or EAL considerations.

The summary continued by exploring how various learning theories provide a framework for these adaptations. Behaviourism, with its focus on structured environments and positive reinforcement, supports students who need consistency. Constructivist approaches, such as peer collaboration and scaffolding, allow students to work within their ZPD. Cognitive strategies like metacognition and retrieval practice help students, particularly those with SEND or lower prior attainment, develop independent learning skills.

For EAL students, language barriers can be mitigated with strategies like visual aids, peer-assisted learning and structured vocabulary instruction, all of which aid in meaningful language acquisition and academic achievement.

Ultimately, successful teaching requires a blended approach that combines different theories to create inclusive learning environments. Regular reflection and collaboration with colleagues are essential to ensure effective planning and delivery for all learners.

REFLECTIVE QUESTIONS:
CHAPTER 10

Reflect on some of the classes you have taught within the schools where you have worked as a teacher and ask yourself some reflective questions as follows.

- Which strategies from each learning theory blend together most effectively to support a wide range of learners needs?

- Where might a blend of specific learning theory strategies not work well together or create confusion in the expectations of a task or activity for learners with specific needs? How might you plan and prepare for this?

━━ FURTHER READING ━━

ITTECF 5.8 High quality teaching for all pupils, including those with SEND, is based on strategies which are often already practised by teachers, and which can be developed through training and support.

The report by Davis, P. et al. (2004), *Teaching Strategies and Approaches for Pupils with Special Educational Needs: A Scoping Study*, explores effective teaching methods for students with special educational needs (SEN), following the *Excellence for All Children* Green Paper (DfEE, 1997), wherein the government placed a focus on inclusive education to support diverse learning needs. Through the report, it was found that there was significant overlap of teaching strategies across SEN categories, with inclusive strategies supporting all learners, suggesting a move away from a separate pedagogy for SEN learners.

From the study three main approaches were identified:

- using behavioural models to develop self-regulation, self-monitoring and improve behaviour through consistent and structured rewards and consequences;

- using social constructivist models to emphasise active learning, interactive problem-solving and collaborative knowledge constructions while also developing their social development and their ability to work with and communicate effectively with their peers and teachers;

- using ecological models where there is a focus on the interplay between learners and their environment, through environmental adaptations such as assistive technology and supporting the learners in engaging more effectively in multisensory learning activities allowing them to access and engage more effectively.

Along with these there was consideration for the need for teachers to incorporate effective meta-cognitive and structured instructional techniques – including modelling, explicit questions and procedural aids – to help support in creating an inclusive learning environment.

━━ REFERENCES ━━

Bada, S. O. (2015). Constructivism learning theory: a paradigm for teaching and learning. *IOSR Journal of Research and Method in Education*, 5(6), 66–70.

Bloom, B. S. (1956). *Taxonomy of Educational Objectives: The Classification of Educational Goals. Handbook I: Cognitive Domain*. Philadelphia, PA: David McKay.

Bourdieu, P. (1986). The forms of capital. In J. Richardson (ed.), *Handbook of Theory and Research for the Sociology of Education*. Westport, CT: Greenwood, pp. 241–58.

Bruner, J. (1966). *Toward a Theory of Instruction*. Cambridge, MA: Harvard University Press.

Davis, P., Florian, L., Ainscow, M., Dyson, A., Farrell, P., Hick, P. and Rouse, M. (2004). *Teaching Strategies and Approaches for Pupils with Special Educational Needs: A Scoping Study* (Research Report No. 516). DfES. https://dera.ioe.ac.uk/6059/1/RR516.pdf

Department for Education (DfE) (2025). *Secondary Accountability Measures: Guide for Maintained Secondary Schools, Academies and Free Schools.* Available at: www.gov.uk/government/publications/progress-8-school-performance-measure/secondary-accountability-measures-2025-guidance-for-maintained-secondary-schools-academies-and-free-schools. Accessed 21 November 2025.

Department for Education and Department of Health (DfE and DoH) (2015). *Special Educational Needs and Disability Code of Practice: 0 to 25 Years.* Available at: https://assets.publishing.service.gov.uk/media/5a7dcb85ed915d2ac884d995/SEND_Code_of_Practice_January_2015.pdf. Accessed 21 November 2025.

Department of Education (DfE), Australian Government (2025). *Students from Low Socio-Economic Areas and STEM Education.* Available at: www.education.gov.au/australian-curriculum/national-stem-education-resources-toolkit/i-want-know-about-stem-education/which-school-students-need-stem-education/students-low-socio-economic-areas. Accessed 21 November 2025.

Department for Education and Employment (DfEE) (1997). *Excellence for All Children.* Available at: www.education-uk.org/documents/pdfs/1997-green-paper.pdf. Accessed 21 November 2025.

Education Endowment Foundation (EEF) (2021). *Metacognition and Self-Regulated Learning: Guidance Report.* Available at: https://educationendowmentfoundation.org.uk/education-evidence/guidance-reports/metacognition. Accessed 21 November 2025.

EEF (2025). *Collaborative Learning Approaches.* Available at: https://educationendowmentfoundation.org.uk/education-evidence/teaching-learning-toolkit/collaborative-learning-approaches. Accessed 21 November 2025.

Flavell, J. H. (1979). Metacognition and cognitive monitoring: a new area of cognitive–developmental inquiry. *American Psychologist, 34*(10), 906–11.

Frayer, D. A., Frederick, W. C. and Klausmeier, H. J. (1969). *A Schema for Testing the Level of Cognitive Mastery.* Madison, WI: Wisconsin Research and Development Center for Cognitive Learning.

Gear, R. (2022). How do children with special educational needs experience retrieval practice? *Chartered College of Teaching.* Available at: https://my.chartered.college/impact_article/how-do-children-with-special-educational-needs-experience-retrieval-practice-2/. Accessed 21 November 2025.

Halliwell, R. (2025). Supporting students with SEMH needs: an exploration of teacher-student relationships and the use of personalised learning approaches. Doctoral thesis, University of Manchester.

Hattie, J. and Timperley, H. (2007). The power of feedback. *Review of Educational Research, 77*(1), 81–112.

Jones, K. (2025). Chunking in the classroom. *Evidence Based Education.* Available at: https://evidence-based.education/resource/chunking-in-the-classroom/. Accessed 21 November 2025.

Karpicke, J. D. and Blunt, J. R. (2011). Retrieval practice produces more learning than elaborative studying with concept mapping. *Science, 331*(6018), 772–5. https://doi.org/10.1126/science.1199327

Leaf, J. B., Cihon, J. H., Leaf, R., McEachin, J. and Taubman, M. (2016). A progressive approach to discrete trial teaching: some current guidelines. *International Electronic Journal of Elementary Education, 9*(2), 361–72.

Lindorff, A., Strand, S. and Au, I. (2025). *English as an Additional Language (EAL) and Educational Achievement in England: An Analysis of Publicly Available Data*. Oxford: Oxford University Press.

Piaget, J. (1950). *The Psychology of Intelligence*. London: Routledge.

The Bell Foundation (2018). *Classroom Support Strategies: Working with EAL Learners in Primary Settings*. Available at: www.bell-foundation.org.uk/app/uploads/2018/07/Classroom-Support-Strategies-Working-with-EAL-Learners-in-Primary-Settings.pdf. Accessed 21 November 2025.

The Bell Foundation (2025). *Language and Learning Loss: The Evidence on Children who use English as an Additional Language*. Available at: www.bell-foundation.org.uk/our-work/with-schools/research/language-and-learning-loss-the-evidence-on-children-who-use-english-as-an-additional-language/. Accessed 21 November 2025.

Vygotsky, L. S. (1978). *Mind in Society: The Development of Higher Psychological Processes*. Cambridge, MA: Harvard University Press.

Wood, D., Bruner, J. S. and Ross, G. (1976). The role of tutoring in problem solving. *Journal of Child Psychology and Psychiatry*, *17*(2), 89–100. https://doi.org/10.1111/j.1469-7610.1976.tb00381.x

Zajda, J. (2021). Constructivist learning theory and creating effective learning environments. In J. Zajda, *Globalisation and Education Reforms*. Heidelberg: Springer, pp. 35–50. https://doi.org/10.1007/978-3-030-76589-8_3

Zimmerman, B. J. (2002). Becoming a self-regulated learner: an overview. *Theory Into Practice*, *41*(2), 64–70. https://doi.org/10.1207/s15430421tip4102_2

11

HOW LEARNING SCIENCES AFFECT ASSESSMENT DESIGN AND PREPARATION FOR ASSESSMENT

LEARNING OUTCOMES

By reading this chapter you will develop:

- An understanding of the principles of effective assessment design
- An understanding that formative assessment strategies are integral to the learning process
- An understanding of how the learning sciences support formative assessment strategies

INITIAL TEACHER TRAINING AND EARLY CAREER FRAMEWORK (ITTECF)

The key readings from the ITTECF that is to be explored within this chapter are:

Black, P. and Wiliam, D. (2009). Developing the theory of formative assessment. *Educational Assessment, Evaluation and Accountability, 21*(1), 5-31. https://doi.org/10.1007/s11092-008-9068-5

Hattie, J. and Timperley, H. (2007). The power of feedback. *Review of Educational Research, 77*(1), 81-112. https://doi.org/10.3102/003465430298487

INTRODUCTION

The focus of this chapter is on how formative assessment strategies can be used to improve learning outcomes. It explores the intersection between learning sciences and assessment, focusing on how principles such as cognitive development, metacognition, motivation and sociocultural learning can guide both the design of assessments and the ways in which students are supported in preparing for them. While summative assessments are a separate or final stage of teaching, we consider formative assessment as an integral part of the learning process that should reinforce understanding, promote reflection and support progress.

ASSESSMENT IN THE SECONDARY SCHOOL

There is no getting away from the fact that secondary school education in England is, ultimately, assessment driven. While as subject teachers we are keen to engender a love of our subject within our students, and endeavour in our lessons to share the joy of finding things out and experience pleasure in honing their skills, the fact remains that at the end of their five years with us, students need to leave with a decent set of summative grades in order to open doors to their future lives, especially if they intend to take our subject further, through college or higher education. Additionally, assessment results do not only impact on the students' future. One of the key indicators of school-wide effectiveness is student performance on standardised tests and overall academic progress, and these results have become a measure of individual teacher effectiveness linked to teacher performance management targets, with heads of department being responsible for the results of entire cohorts, not just their own classes. This can lead to a very stressful relationship with assessments, culminating towards the end of Year 11, when students are preparing for their final exam preparation and teachers' rising stress levels are palpable. This is a situation to be avoided as we already know from our work on learning sciences of the detrimental effect of stress on learning (Howard-Jones, 2018).

To mitigate the effects of the stress of final preparations and last-minute cramming, assessment opportunities are mapped onto long-term plans and built into medium-term plans and individual lesson plans across the year groups. These can take the form of half-termly assessments of units of work throughout Key Stage 3 and Key Stage 4 as well as continued low-stakes checking of learning throughout lessons. These regular assessments should mean that students are familiarised with the routines and behavioural aspects of testing, lowering the stress associated with them, and will have had many opportunities to retrieve and consolidate learning prior to the final summative assessment.

Formative assessment, often used interchangeably with *assessment for learning* (AfL), is a key aspect of assessment practice in the secondary school. It refers to any assessment activities undertaken by teachers and students that provide feedback, which is then used to adapt teaching methods to meet student needs and improve learning outcomes. The theoretical understanding of formative assessment has evolved significantly, building on the foundational work of Black and Wiliam (1998), who gathered a wide range of research findings which unequivocally demonstrated that improving formative assessment raises student achievement, a conclusion supported by over 250 research articles. This positive finding naturally led to the question of how to improve formative assessment, which initially lacked detailed practical guidance. Subsequent efforts aimed to provide a unifying basis for diverse formative practices and move beyond a mere list of activities to a coherent rationale

(Black and Wiliam, 2009). This progression also emphasised the need to locate formative interactions within more comprehensive theories of pedagogy, focusing on theoretical models of learning and its regulation, where feedback is just one element.

FORMATIVE ASSESSMENT STRATEGIES (BLACK AND WILIAM'S FRAMEWORK)

Based on earlier research, Black and Wiliam identified five key strategies that conceptualise effective formative assessment:

1. *clarifying and sharing learning intentions and criteria for success*: students must understand what they are expected to learn and what successful completion looks like. This empowers them to work towards goals;

2. *engineering effective classroom discussions and other learning tasks that elicit evidence of student understanding*: teachers need to design tasks and questions that reveal student thinking, moving beyond simple factual recall. This involves allowing adequate 'wait time' after questions, encouraging brainstorming and engaging in *interpretive listening* to understand students' reasoning;

3. *providing feedback that moves learners forward*: feedback is most effective when it is primarily comments-only, avoids numerical scores or grades (which can lead students to ignore the comments) and is designed to make students think about their work. It should identify what was done well, what needs improvement and guide how to make that improvement;

4. *activating students as instructional resources for one another (peer assessment)*: by assessing and providing feedback to their peers, students develop critical judgement, objectivity and a deeper understanding of success criteria. This also helps them learn from alternative perspectives expressed in the language of their peers;

5. *activating students as the owners of their own learning (self-assessment)*: this is essential for learning, requiring students to understand learning goals, monitor their own progress and take responsibility for their learning. It involves developing metacognitive skills to manage and control their own work. Tools like 'traffic light' icons can facilitate self-assessment and communication of understanding.

It can be seen that these deceptively simple strategies align closely with several foundational principles from the learning sciences. The emphasis on dialogue, peer interaction and scaffolding reflects Vygotsky's idea that learning is socially mediated and supports the idea that learners construct knowledge actively, rather than passively receiving information.

Effective formative assessment helps manage cognitive load by identifying misconceptions early and adjusting instruction accordingly; encouraging students to reflect on their own learning and use feedback to adjust strategies aligns with research on metacognition.

Additionally, formative assessment practices that emphasise autonomy, competence and relatedness can enhance intrinsic motivation. Crucially, Black and Wiliam posit that assessment should be responsive to where students are in their development.

THE ROLE OF FEEDBACK (HATTIE AND TIMPERLEY'S MODEL)

Hattie and Timperley (2007) provide a comprehensive model of feedback, defining it as information provided by an agent (e.g., teacher, peer, book, parent, experience) regarding aspects of one's performance or understanding. A synthesis of over 500 meta-analyses reported by Hattie (1999) found that the average effect of schooling on student achievement was 0.40. In contrast, the average effect size for feedback from 12 meta-analyses (196 studies, 6,972 effect sizes) was 0.79, placing it among the top five to ten highest influences on achievement. However, the effect sizes show considerable variability, indicating that the type and delivery of feedback significantly influence its effectiveness. Studies with the highest effect sizes involved students receiving information about a task and how to perform it more effectively. Lower effect sizes were associated with praise, rewards and punishment. Hattie and Timperley suggest that effective feedback aims to reduce discrepancies between current understandings/performance and a learning goal, and should address three major questions.

• Where am I going? (What are the goals and success criteria?)

• How am I going? (What progress is being made?)

• Where to next? (What activities are needed for better progress?)

Hattie and Timperley categorise feedback into four levels, each with differential effectiveness:

1. *feedback about the task* (FT): focuses on whether work is correct or incorrect, or acquiring more information (e.g., 'You need to include more about the Treaty of Versailles'). This is the most common type and is powerful when addressing faulty interpretations rather than a complete lack of information. Written comments are significantly more effective than grades alone for this level;

2. *feedback about the processing of the task* (FP): concerns the processes or strategies used to create a product or complete a task (e.g., 'You need to edit this piece of writing by attending to the descriptors you have used ...'). This level is more effective for enhancing deeper learning than FT, as it helps students detect errors and apply better strategies;

3. *feedback about self-regulation* (FR): focuses on the learner's self-monitoring, directing and regulating actions (e.g., 'You already know the key features of the opening of an argument. Check to see whether you have incorporated them ...'). This is powerful for deep processing and mastery as it encourages students to develop self-efficacy, self-assessment and help-seeking skills. Effective learners naturally generate internal feedback;

4. *feedback about the self as a person* (FS): expresses positive (or negative) evaluations about the student personally (e.g., 'Good girl', 'Great effort'). This level is least effective as it typically contains little task-related information and can deflect attention from the task. Praise, in particular, often has little relationship to student achievement and can even be counterproductive, potentially damaging self-esteem or promoting an ego-oriented rather than task-oriented approach.

The timing of feedback is also critical, varying by the level and complexity of the task. Immediate feedback may be more powerful for task acquisition, while some delay can be beneficial for complex tasks requiring deeper processing. Both positive and negative feedback can be beneficial, but their effectiveness depends on the level at which they are aimed and processed, and a student's self-efficacy. A supportive classroom climate is crucial, where errors are viewed as opportunities for learning, reducing the personal risk students feel when responding publicly.

Hattie and Timperley's feedback model (2007) aligns strongly with several key principles from the learning sciences, particularly in its exploration of how feedback influences learning outcomes. The model emphasises that feedback should reduce the gap between current and desired performance, which aligns with cognitive theories of learning that focus on information processing and schema development. Feedback that clarifies goals and provides cues for improvement supports learners in refining mental models and correcting misconceptions. Encouraging reflection and goal setting helps students monitor and regulate their own learning strategies, while feedback focused on effort and strategies (rather than ability or outcomes) supports self-regulation and encourages persistence. Additionally, feedback is framed as a dialogic process, not just transmission of information, which reflects Vygotsky's view that learning is mediated through social interaction where peer and teacher feedback can scaffold learning within the learner's zone of proximal development (ZPD).

INTEGRATED FORMATIVE ASSESSMENT AND PEDAGOGICAL THEORY

The five key formative assessment strategies outlined by Black and Wiliam naturally integrate with Hattie and Timperley's feedback model:

- clarifying and sharing learning intentions and criteria for success directly addresses Hattie and Timperley's 'Where am I going?' question, ensuring students have clear goals;

- engineering effective classroom discussions and learning tasks elicits evidence of understanding, providing the basis for feedback that answers 'How am I going?' and 'Where to next?' at the task and process levels;

- providing feedback that moves learners forward is the direct application of Hattie and Timperley's insights, focusing on comments-only feedback at the task, process and self-regulation levels to encourage deeper thinking and improvement;

- activating students as instructional resources for one another (peer assessment) and activating students as owners of their own learning (self-assessment) are crucial for fostering self-regulation and for providing feedback at the process level through collaborative learning. This also aligns with Vygotsky's principle of ideas appearing first in the external social plane before internalisation.

The very definition of formative assessment, where evidence is 'elicited, interpreted, and used by teachers, learners, or their peers, to make decisions about the next steps in instruction that are likely to be better, or better founded' (Black and Wiliam, 2009: 9), is inherently a feedback loop aimed at reducing discrepancies and moving learning forward.

VALIDITY AND CONSTRUCTS IN ASSESSMENT

A key development in assessment theory is the understanding that validity is a property of inferences made from assessments, rather than an inherent property of the assessments themselves. This has led to the consensus that *construct* interpretations must be at the heart of all assessments (Wiliam, 2010).

A construct is defined as a hypothesised attribute of individuals, assumed to be reflected in test performance. It possesses predictive properties, and its meaning is given by the network of laws and relationships (the *nomological net*) in which it occurs. More specifically, a construct is an ability – that is, a human characteristic required for successful task performance that differentiates successful from unsuccessful performance and applies to some tasks but not others.

TWO PRIMARY THREATS TO THE VALIDITY OF CONSTRUCT INTERPRETATIONS

* *Construct under-representation*: occurs when an assessment is too narrow and fails to adequately represent all aspects of the intended construct. For instance, a multiple-choice test for history might effectively assess knowledge of *facts* and *dates*, but significantly under-represent the construct of *interpreting evidence*.

* *Construct-irrelevant variance*: occurs when an assessment introduces extraneous factors unrelated to the construct of interest into the scores – for example, an essay test designed to assess historical knowledge might inadvertently measure a student's writing ability or handwriting quality, thereby introducing construct-irrelevant variance.

Many debates surrounding the adequacy and appropriateness of assessments are, at their core, debates about construct definition and construct choice rather than purely technical issues of assessment design. Wiliam (2010) argues that these definitional debates should precede the design of the assessment itself, and involve a broader public, not just assessment experts, to prevent what is easy, practicable, or inexpensive to assess from unduly influencing the definition of what is important.

CORE PRINCIPLES FOR ASSESSMENT DESIGN

Pelligrino et al. (2016) address the lack of discussion on the design and validation of assessments used close to classroom teaching and learning, and present a framework for conceptualising and organising the multiple components of validity applicable to these classroom-level assessments. The authors suggest the core principles for assessment design can be understood through two main frameworks: the *assessment triangle* and *construct-centred design*.

THE ASSESSMENT TRIANGLE

Assessments are tools to observe student behaviour and produce data that can be used to draw reasonable inferences about what students know. This process involves a chain of reasoning about student learning from evidence and is conceptualised by the assessment triangle, which has three interconnected elements:

- *cognition*: this refers to theories, models, data and assumptions about how students represent knowledge and develop competence in a subject matter domain. A theory of learning is needed to identify the important knowledge and skills to measure, representing the most scientifically credible understanding of how learners develop expertise. This forms the foundation for arguments related to an assessment's cognitive validity;

- *observation*: this involves a set of assumptions and principles about the kinds of tasks or situations that will elicit observable evidence of students' knowledge and skills. Tasks must be carefully designed to provide evidence linked to the cognitive model and support the intended inferences;

- *interpretation*: this encompasses the methods and tools used to reason from observations to make sense of the evidence. It characterises the inferential validity of the assessment, explaining how observations provide information relative to the cognitive model and instructional implications.

For an assessment to be effective and valid, these three elements must be in synchrony.

LEARNING PROGRESSIONS

Assessments should be grounded in models of learning that describe how students typically progress in understanding over time. These progressions help teachers design tasks that are developmentally appropriate and diagnostically useful. Pellegrino et al. (2016) suggest that the targets of inference for an assessment (i.e., 'what knowledge and skills are being reasoned about') should be largely determined by models of cognition and learning that describe how people represent knowledge and develop competence in a domain. These models, often in the form of learning progressions (or learning trajectories), are empirically grounded and testable hypotheses about how students' understanding and ability to use core concepts and disciplinary practices grow and become more sophisticated over time with instruction. The authors argue that effective assessments should be aligned with an empirically grounded cognitive model which should include:

- *target performances or learning goals*: the end points of the progression;

- *progress variables*: dimensions of understanding and application tracked over time;

- *levels of achievement*: intermediate steps in the developmental pathways;

- *learning performances*: the kinds of tasks students at a particular level would be capable of performing;

- *assessments*: specific measures used to track student development along the progression.

CONSTRUCT-CENTRED DESIGN

Assessment tasks should be developed using a structured approach that begins with defining the construct, identifying the evidence needed to support claims about student learning and designing tasks that elicit that evidence. Unlike traditional approaches that focus on surface features of tasks, construct-centred design guides the selection and development of assessment tasks, scoring rubrics and reporting styles by the construct itself and the best ways to elicit evidence about a student's proficiency with that construct. This approach aligns closely with the assessment triangle's emphasis on evidentiary reasoning. Key developmental steps in construct-centred design include:

- analysing the cognitive domain;

- specifying the constructs to be assessed in detailed language to guide task design;

- identifying the inferences the assessment should support;

- laying out the type of evidence needed to support those inferences;

- designing tasks to collect that evidence and modelling how the evidence can be assembled and used to reach valid conclusions;

- iterating through these stages to refine elements as new evidence becomes available.

The process starts by defining precise claims about student knowledge, using specific cognitive verbs (e.g., compare, describe, analyse) rather than vague terms (e.g., know, understand). These claims are then linked to evidence statements that capture the features of work products or performances supporting the claims. This precision then informs the design of tasks and scoring rubrics. Validity is a guiding principle and involves ensuring that the interpretations and uses of assessment results are supported by theory and evidence, and that assessments measure what they intend to measure.

BEST PRACTICE FOR DESIGNING ASSESSMENTS IN SECONDARY SCHOOL (PELLEGRINO ET AL.'S FRAMEWORK)

Pelligrino et al. (2016) argue that effective assessment design, especially for assessments used close to classroom teaching and learning, should be guided by a robust framework that considers validity, cognitive principles and instructional alignment. This means that teachers should consider the following five principles when designing assessment tasks for use in the classroom.

1. *Focus on validity*: the validity of an assessment is an argument consisting of claims about its intended interpretive use and the evidence supporting those claims. Pelligrino et al. (2016) suggest that for classroom-level assessments, three components are particularly salient:
   - *cognitive validity*: this addresses how well an assessment taps into important domain knowledge and skills without being confounded by other cognitive aspects, and how well it reflects scientific understanding of student cognition and its development;
   - *instructional validity*: this component concerns the alignment of the assessment with the curriculum and instruction, including students' opportunities to learn, and its ability to provide valuable, timely information that supports teaching practice;

- *inferential validity*: this relates to the extent an assessment reliably and accurately provides model-based information about student performance, particularly for diagnostic purposes. It is closely linked to cognitive and instructional validity claims.

Pelligrino et al. (2016) argue that for an assessment to be valid and effective, evidence for each component should be collected from multiple, complementary sources.

2. *Construct-centred design*: assessments should be developed using a construct-centred approach. This involves:

   - defining the cognitive domain and specifying the constructs to be assessed in detailed language to guide task design;
   - identifying the inferences the assessment should support and specifying the type of evidence needed for those inferences;
   - designing tasks to collect that evidence and modelling how it will be used to reach valid conclusions.

The aim is to ensure that assessment tasks clearly reveal students' knowledge and understanding, making inferences about student cognition unambiguous. The assessment triangle (cognition, observation, interpretation) highlights how these elements must be in synchrony for an assessment to be effective and valid.

3. *Align with learning progressions*: assessment design should be informed by learning progressions, which are empirically grounded hypotheses about how students' understanding and abilities develop over time with instruction. This helps structure claims about tasks and contributes to arguments about cognitive, instructional and inferential validity.

4. *Depth of knowledge* (DoK): assessments should aim for varying levels of cognitive demand. While tasks involving recall and reproduction (DoK Level 1) are common, it's crucial to include items that require skills and concepts (DoK Level 2) and strategic thinking (DoK Level 3) to assess deeper learning. For instance, Pelligrino at al.'s (2016) analysis of elementary mathematics assessments found a majority of items were at DoK Level 1, limiting their diagnostic capacity.

5. *Reduce administrative burden*: the design of assessment and reporting requirements should minimise unnecessary and unproductive tasks for teachers. Excessive detail and duplication in recording, inputting, monitoring and analysing data, as well as frequent and poorly timed data requests, significantly burden teachers and detract from valuable planning time. Solutions include delegating administrative duties, improving and integrating IT systems, and reducing the frequency and detail of reporting.

CRITICISM OF ASSESSMENT

While formative assessment is widely supported by robust research and underpinned by well-established theoretical frameworks, its practical application and evaluation continue to face persistent challenges. These can be broadly grouped into three categories: implementation and practice, assessment design and validity, and the measurement of impact.

CHALLENGES IN IMPLEMENTATION AND PRACTICE

One of the most frequently cited concerns by teachers is the significant workload associated with implementing formative assessment effectively. The demands of detailed documentation, repeated data entry across multiple platforms and time-consuming marking often exceed the time available. This is particularly evident during peak periods, such as when Year 11 students undertake mock exams. In these instances, marking must align closely with examination board criteria to ensure feedback is both accurate and useful, adding further pressure to already stretched schedules.

Moreover, although formative assessment strategies are supported by clear guidelines, their application often varies considerably between schools. Local adaptations, shaped by institutional context and prior experience, can lead to divergent interpretations of what formative assessment entails. Teachers and lead practitioners may differ in their understanding, resulting in practices that stray from the original design. Training is sometimes viewed as overly theoretical, with a stronger emphasis on research than on practical classroom implementation. Many teachers express a preference for more interactive, hands-on training that addresses real-world challenges and supports flexible adaptation of strategies. A disconnect can also arise between the prescriptive nature of initial training and the more nuanced guidance offered during ongoing programme delivery.

Creating a classroom environment where students are open to feedback, especially when it involves correction or disconfirmation, is another key challenge. Students may perceive public errors as risky, making them reluctant to engage. Older students, particularly those focused on exams, can be sceptical of formative techniques such as peer assessment, often favouring direct teacher input. Additionally, the tension between formative and summative assessment remains unresolved. While some argue for a clear separation to avoid the distorting effects of high-stakes testing, in practice, this division is difficult to maintain. School policies that require grades on every assignment can further limit the use of comments-only feedback, undermining the formative process.

CHALLENGES IN ASSESSMENT DESIGN AND VALIDITY

Despite its importance, the design and validation of classroom-based assessments have historically received limited attention. Assessment development is often fragmented, resulting in tools that inadequately represent the intended constructs, lack comprehensive content coverage and offer limited inferential scope. Many curriculum materials include assessments with little or no supporting validity evidence.

At the heart of many debates around assessment lies the issue of construct definition; what exactly is being measured? Without a clear starting point, assessments risk being shaped by what is easiest, most practical, or least costly to measure, rather than what is most meaningful. This can lead to construct under-representation (assessments that are too narrow) or construct-irrelevant variance (assessments influenced by unrelated factors, such as writing ability in a history test). Even small accommodations can inadvertently shift the construct being assessed.

Assessments also carry the risk of distortion, as described by Campbell's Law. When assessment outcomes are used for decision-making, such as evaluating school or individual teacher's performance, they can become targets themselves, subject to manipulation and corruption. Over time, schools may adjust practices to optimise scores rather than improve learning, altering the relationship between assessment outcomes and actual educational quality. Furthermore, even technically valid assessments can be ethically problematic if they rely on construct definitions that disadvantage certain groups.

LIMITATIONS IN MEASURING IMPACT

Assessing genuine learning remains a complex endeavour. Teachers may rely on superficial indicators of progress rather than seeking direct, valid evidence of deep understanding. Learning is often misconstrued as passive knowledge acquisition, whereas formative assessment aims to support active knowledge construction. Many commonly used classroom assessments fail to promote meaningful learning, and feedback is frequently vague, overly focused on praise, or lacking in actionable guidance.

The effectiveness of feedback varies widely depending on its nature, timing and delivery. While certain strategies, such as metacognitive approaches and targeted feedback, show promise, the supporting evidence is sometimes limited in scope or relevance, making it difficult to generalise findings to broader educational contexts.

Finally, despite the widespread adoption of formative assessment practices such as AfL in England, national learning outcomes have shown little sustained improvement. This paradox highlights the gap between advocating high-impact strategies and achieving consistent, scalable implementation. The absence of systematic, high-quality data on pupil attainment further complicates efforts to evaluate progress. Teachers often believe that the benefits of formative assessment take time to manifest, particularly in relation to high-stakes exams like GCSEs. As a result, short-term evaluations may underestimate its true impact.

In summary, while the theoretical foundations of formative assessment are compelling, translating these into consistent, effective and measurable practice across diverse educational settings remains a complex and ongoing challenge.

PRACTICAL APPLICATION

As a student or early career teacher, it is likely that you will be asked to administer and mark assessments that have already been prepared by more knowledgeable others in your department; later on you will become familiar with the *assessment objectives* (AOs) of the subject GCSEs.

CASE STUDY: BEST PRACTICES FOR PREPARING STUDENTS FOR ASSESSMENT IN SECONDARY SCHOOL

Effective assessment preparation is not a one-off event; it's a continuous process woven into everyday teaching and is most effective when it draws on multiple learning sciences. This case study explores how secondary teachers can support students in becoming confident, reflective learners who are well prepared for both formative and summative assessments. By now you will be able to recognise the elements of the learning sciences that are interwoven with the strategies described and, as such, we have not thought it necessary to spell them out in this case study.

CLARIFYING LEARNING INTENTIONS AND SUCCESS CRITERIA

At the heart of successful assessment preparation is clarity. Students need to understand what they are learning and how success will be measured. For example, in a Year 10 English class, the teacher began each unit by co-constructing success criteria with students. This was achieved by reviewing the examination board AOs and putting them into student-friendly language. Using model texts to illustrate key features of each AO helped students visualise what high-quality work looked like and gave them a clear roadmap for improvement. By revisiting these criteria throughout the unit, students were able to monitor their own progress and take ownership of their learning.

ENGINEERING EFFECTIVE CLASSROOM DISCUSSIONS AND ACTIVITIES

The teacher used open-ended questions like 'How do we know the writer's intent?' to spark curiosity and deeper thinking. Wait time was increased after asking questions, allowing students to reflect before responding. Even 'I'm not sure' answers were welcomed, creating a safe space for exploration and allowing the opportunity for dialogic teaching, where other students were invited to contribute. Collaborative tasks encouraged students to share ideas and challenge each other respectfully, building a classroom culture where dialogue supported learning.

Key strategies included:

- using 'big questions' to frame lessons;
- encouraging students to explain their reasoning;
- designing group activities that promote discussion and evaluation.

PROVIDING FEEDBACK THAT MOVES LEARNERS FORWARD

Feedback is most powerful when it's specific, actionable and timely. In this class, the teacher used comment-only marking on mock exam papers. Students received feedback on what they did well, what needed improvement and how to improve. They then spent a lesson revising their answers using *comment sheets* to track their responses. This approach to self-regulated learning (SRL) helped students engage with feedback meaningfully and improved their confidence.

Effective feedback practices used:

- focus on comments rather than grades;
- address three key questions: Where am I going? How am I doing? Where to next?
- target feedback at task, process and self-regulation levels;
- create time for students to respond and revise;
- foster a climate where mistakes are seen as learning opportunities.

While generic formative assessment skills apply across subjects, subject-specific pedagogical content knowledge is vital for interpreting student responses and formulating effective questions and feedback.

The nature of 'open' versus 'closed' tasks varies by subject (e.g., writing a poem vs solving a maths problem), requiring nuanced assessment approaches.

ACTIVATING STUDENTS AS INSTRUCTIONAL RESOURCES FOR ONE ANOTHER

Peer assessment can be a powerful tool when structured well. In this class, students used simplified rubrics to assess each other's essays. They discussed strengths and areas for improvement in pairs, using everyday language that felt accessible. They were encouraged to only comment on the aspect of the AO under consideration (i.e., the relevant construct, not being distracted by commenting on, for example, handwriting or spellings). This activity not only improved their understanding of the criteria, but also helped them reflect on their own work more objectively.

ACTIVATING STUDENTS AS OWNERS OF THEIR OWN LEARNING

Self-assessment encouraged students to take responsibility for their progress. Students used 'traffic lights' to rate their understanding of key concepts. They then worked in groups to justify their ratings and plan their revision sessions, using interleaving. This simple SRL strategy helped students become more aware of their learning needs and develop metacognitive skills. The teacher provided links to suitable online revision sites and encouraged students to share and discuss any other online resources they had used, so that they could be confident they were not being fed disinformation that could skew their understanding.

FORMATIVE USE OF SUMMATIVE TESTS

Summative assessments were used formatively. In the Year 10 revision session, students reviewed past test papers and traffic-lighted topics based on their confidence levels. They created their own revision questions and marked each other's answers, identifying common misconceptions. This approach turned testing into a learning opportunity and helped students prepare more effectively.

CONCLUSION

New teachers should be aware that younger students often embrace formative assessment more readily than older, exam-focused learners. Embedding these practices early and consistently helps build a culture of reflection and resilience. Preparing students for assessment is not just about test readiness; it's about equipping them with the skills to learn deeply and independently.

CONSIDER THIS: ASSESSMENT

Considering the idea that most approaches to teaching and learning blend ideas from multiple learning sciences, reflect on the ideas pertaining to assessment presented in this chapter. In reflecting on this, think about:

- how different learning theories influence the design and use of formative assessment in your class-room. Consider how these perspectives shape your understanding of feedback, student engagement and the role of assessment in learning;

- what practical barriers you might face when implementing formative assessment strategies and how could you adapt your approach to overcome them. Reflect on workload, time constraints and school policies that may affect your ability to use assessment effectively;

- the ways in which assessment can be designed unintentionally to misrepresent what students know or can do. Think about issues like construct validity, assessment bias and the influence of external factors (e.g., language proficiency, test format) on student performance;

- how you can ensure that feedback leads to meaningful learning rather than confusion or discourage-ment. Reflect on the timing, clarity and focus of feedback and how it supports students in developing metacognitive skills and ownership of their learning.

CHAPTER SUMMARY

This chapter underscored that formative assessment is an integral component of the learning process, moving beyond a final stage to continuously reinforce understanding, promote reflection and support student progress. It was grounded in influential theoretical frameworks, notably Black and Wiliam's five key strategies. These include clarifying learning intentions, engineering effective classroom discussions to elicit understanding, providing actionable feedback and activating students as both peer assessors and owners of their own learning.

Complementing this is Hattie and Timperley's comprehensive feedback model, which defines feedback as information used to reduce discrepancies between current performance and learning goals. Effective feedback, highly influential on achievement, addresses three core questions: 'Where am I going?', 'How am I going?' and 'Where to next?' It is categorised into four levels: task, process, self-regulation and self as a person, with feedback about self-regulation being particularly powerful for deep learning. Both frameworks align strongly with learning science principles, supporting the idea that learning is socially mediated and that feedback, dialogue and self-reflection enhance metacognition and intrinsic motivation.

A crucial learning point is the centrality of validity and construct definition in assessment design. Assessments must accurately represent the intended construct, the specific ability or knowledge being measured, to avoid construct under-representation (assessments being too narrow) or con-struct-irrelevant variance (measuring unrelated factors). Pellegrino et al.'s assessment triangle (cognition, observation, interpretation) and construct-centred design provide a structured approach to ensure assessments are robust, evidence-based and yield valid inferences about student learning.

Despite this strong theoretical foundation, the chapter acknowledges persistent challenges in practi-cal application. These include significant teacher workload, inconsistencies in implementation and difficulties in fostering a classroom culture where students genuinely welcome feedback and errors. Measuring the actual impact on national learning outcomes also remains complex. Ultimately, the chapter advocates for assessment preparation as a continuous, integrated process within everyday teaching, applying these design principles to foster deep, independent learning.

REFLECTIVE QUESTIONS: CHAPTER 11

Think about a recent assessment you have been involved with administering and marking.

- What were the constructs (skills and attributes) the assessment was designed to measure?

- How was the evidence about a student's proficiency with that construct gathered to reach valid conclusions?

- Were there any examples of construct-irrelevant variance - that is, extraneous factors unrelated to the construct of interest being introduced into the scores?

— FURTHER READING

ITTECF 6.1: Effective assessment is critical to teaching because it provides teachers with information about pupils' understanding and needs.

Christodoulou, D. (2017). *Making Good Progress: The Future of Assessment for Learning.* Oxford: Oxford University Press.

Christodoulou critiques the dominant assessment practices in English schools, particularly the use of national curriculum levels, arguing that they have distorted teaching and learning. She contends that these levels were based on flawed assumptions about how students learn and progress, leading to superficial lesson structures and ineffective assessment tasks.

Drawing on cognitive science and her experience at Ark schools, Christodoulou proposes a clearer distinction between formative and summative assessment. She argues that formative assessment should be frequent, low stakes and focused on specific elements of the curriculum to guide teaching and support learning. In contrast, summative assessment should be standardised, broad in scope and used to make valid comparisons across students and schools.

The book challenges the idea that all assessment should be based on generic skills or descriptors, advocating instead for domain-specific knowledge and practice. Ultimately, she calls for a more research-informed approach to assessment, one that supports deep learning, reduces teacher workload and aligns more closely with how students actually learn.

— REFERENCES

Black, P. and Wiliam, D. (1998). *Inside the Black Box: Raising Standards Through Classroom Assessment.* Brentford: Granada Learning.

Black, P. and Wiliam, D. (2009). Developing the theory of formative assessment. *Educational Assessment, Evaluation and Accountability, 21*(1), 5–31. https://doi.org/10.1007/s11092-008-9068-5

Hattie, J. (1999). *Influences on Student Learning.* Inaugural professorial address, University of Auckland, New Zealand. Available at: https://geoffpetty.com/wp-content/uploads/2012/12/Influencesonstudent2C683.pdf. Accessed 21 November 2025.

Hattie, J. and Timperley, H. (2007). The power of feedback. *Review of Educational Research, 77*(1), 81–112. https://doi.org/10.3102/003465430298487

Howard-Jones, P. (2018). *Evolution of the Learning Brain: Or How You Got to be So Smart ...* London: Routledge.

Pellegrino, J. W., DiBello, L. V. and Goldman, S. R. (2016). A framework for conceptualizing and evaluating the validity of instructionally relevant assessments. *Educational Psychologist, 51*(1), 59–81.

Wiliam, D. (2010). What counts as evidence of educational achievement? The role of constructs in the pursuit of equity in assessment. *Review of Research in Education, 34*, 254–84. https://doi.org/10.3102/0091732X09351544

PART 4

12

REFLECTIONS AND SPECULATION ON THE FUTURE OF LEARNING SCIENCES IN TEACHING

LEARNING OUTCOMES

By reading this chapter you will:

- Reflect on your critical understanding of how learning sciences inform current pedagogical practices in secondary education
- Consider emerging trends and technologies in education through the lens of learning sciences, considering both their potential and limitations
- Reflect on the ethical implications of applying learning sciences in diverse educational contexts, with attention to equity, data privacy and teacher agency

INITIAL TEACHER TRAINING AND EARLY CAREER FRAMEWORK (ITTECF)

The key reading from the ITTECF that is to be explored within this chapter is:

Education Endowment Foundation (EEF) (2024). *Using Research Evidence: A Concise Guide*. https://educationendowmentfoundation.org.uk/support-for-schools/using-research-evidence

INTRODUCTION

The landscape of school-based learning, including classrooms, drama studios and playing fields, is undergoing rapid transformation as our understanding of student learning continually evolves. The authors' previous experiences as teachers included the imposed concept of differentiated work, a practice now recognised to have a detrimental impact on student well-being and progress, in addition to placing a considerable burden on teachers to create multiple resources. Furthermore, we were expected to implement professional development focused on pupils' 'learning styles', a pedagogical approach that has since been largely unsubstantiated by research.

We taught using the overhead projector (OHP), moving on to the interactive whiteboard (IWB) – in the early days nothing more than a glorified projector until teachers learned how to use the software of Smartboard™ or Prometheus™ properly. The similarity with the rise of the learning sciences here is salient; we all had an IWB, but initially did not understand how to use them properly – largely because good practice had not been established or disseminated through high-quality training. But once we had had training and developed confidence in how to use them properly, they became a valuable tool that transformed our practice. Now, classroom teaching is unrecognisable from those days of the OHP and we have never looked back. The learning sciences can be viewed in the same way. For example, metacognitive strategies have become more prominent in secondary classrooms due to learning sciences research. Teachers know that these strategies exist, but might be unsure of how they should be used to best support teaching and learning. However, with proper understanding, using learning sciences to support our teaching can have a transformative effect on our students. We hope this book has supported your understanding of the learning sciences and that, as a result, you will be more confident in your application of them to all aspects of your teaching.

Your greater understanding of how the learning sciences can be blended to support teaching will also have an impact on your own learning as a teacher. You will recognise that the problems with working memory overload also apply to you as you develop your skills and strategies in the new and unfamiliar classroom environment and learn how to manage multiple demands at once. As your subject schema develop so you will become more confident with teaching new topics and, as you grow more familiar with the school routines and behaviour policies, you will develop your own ways of managing them that begin to feel natural to you and get more comfortable as you gain experience. You will collaborate with your fellow teachers in order to gain greater understanding of how to best teach certain aspects of your subject and will develop your own methods of using AI and technology to support your knowledge acquisition and development as a teacher.

In doing all of this, as teachers, you will also be reflecting on current practices and asking yourself whether the way things are done are the best ways; you will anticipate future developments in secondary education, as teaching and our understanding of how people learn best inevitably continues to evolve. There is no escaping the rise of AI and how this will be transformative to the learning of your students. AI can help them revise cued recall, it can help them develop their knowledge for near and far transfer, it can adapt to the cognitive load present in the student, it can converse and help them socially construct new knowledge or just simply help them construct new knowledge to their schema. When AI falls down, that will be where you step in, adapting, helping them create new behaviourist routines and other approaches founded on the blending of learning sciences. AI will not replace the teachers; it will replace some of the work of teachers and free up teachers to do the skilful teaching that needs a human touch.

LEARNING SCIENCES IN SECONDARY EDUCATION TODAY

In this section, we reflect on how learning sciences are currently shaping secondary school practice, the extent of their integration and the challenges that remain. The learning sciences have increasingly influenced secondary education over the past two decades, offering evidence-informed strategies that enhance teaching and learning. Drawing from cognitive psychology and educational research, this interdisciplinary field has helped teachers better understand how students learn and how teaching can be adapted to support that process. Bransford et al. (2000) emphasise the importance of connecting new knowledge to prior understanding, fostering metacognitive awareness and creating learning environments that support active engagement and social interaction. Furthermore, they argue that effective learning environments are built on three key principles:

- *learner-centredness*: recognising and building on students' existing knowledge and experiences;

- *knowledge-centredness*: focusing on deep understanding rather than superficial coverage (think near and far transfer);

- *assessment-centredness*: using formative assessment to guide learning and teaching.

These principles have become central to many contemporary pedagogical approaches in secondary education, particularly those informed by the learning sciences. They also underpin the rationale for integrating strategies such as retrieval practice, spaced learning and metacognitive reflection into classroom practice.

EVIDENCE-INFORMED PEDAGOGIES

One of the most visible impacts of the learning sciences in secondary education is the adoption of cognitive science principles in classroom practice. Techniques such as retrieval practice, spaced repetition and dual coding have gained traction, supported by research demonstrating their effectiveness in improving long-term retention and understanding (Dunlosky et al., 2013). For example, many teachers now incorporate low-stakes quizzes at the start of lessons to activate prior knowledge and reinforce learning, an approach grounded in retrieval practice. However, if these low-stakes quizzes are not repeated, varied or related to the lesson's content they could be counterproductive. In addition, if they are redundant because the class is already 'expert' then it could create an effect called *expert reversal*. For instance, requiring a group of A-level physics students who have already demonstrated mastery of Newton's laws to repeatedly recall the fundamental equations in a series of introductory quizzes may hinder their progress on more complex problem-solving tasks as it diverts valuable time and cognitive effort away from new, challenging material and distracts them from higher-order work.

The Education Endowment Foundation (EEF) has played a pivotal role in translating research into practice in the UK. Its guide to using *research evidence* (2024) is designed to support teachers in understanding, identifying, examining and applying research evidence to inform and develop practice. The guide provides a definition of research evidence and outlines various research types, their uses and potential limitations. Additionally, it provides strategies to assess the quality and reliability of research evidence, urging teachers to 'sense check' findings with their own expertise, critically test the validity and reliability of the evidence and use their professional judgement about how and when to make changes to practice to truly improve pupil outcomes. Ultimately, the guide stresses that while research evidence offers excellent insights it is the teacher's responsibility to use their professional judgement and expertise to make evidence-informed decisions about what will work best to support their students.

PROFESSIONAL DEVELOPMENT AND TEACHER LEARNING

The integration of learning sciences into teacher professional development (CPD) has also grown. Increasingly, CPD programmes are designed to be research-informed, focusing on how teachers can apply cognitive principles in subject-specific contexts. Resources such as the EEF's *Teaching and Learning Toolkit* (2021), which synthesises evidence on strategies such as metacognition, feedback and collaborative learning, provides accessible guidance for teachers – for example, the EEF's report on metacognition and self-regulated learning (2018) has encouraged schools to embed reflective strategies into lessons, helping students become more aware of their own learning processes. Initiatives such as *research schools* and *evidence-based teaching networks* have helped bridge the gap between theory and practice, fostering communities of teachers who engage critically with research. However, the uptake of learning sciences in CPD is uneven. While some schools embrace evidence-informed practice, others struggle due to time constraints, lack of access to high-quality training, or competing priorities. Moreover, the translation of research into practice is not always straightforward; teachers must interpret findings within the realities of their classrooms, which vary widely in terms of student needs, curriculum demands and institutional culture. Sometimes, schools rely on in-house expertise to deliver CPD about applying research from cognitive science into schools. Such in-house 'experts' may not have a strong concept of limitations or the full range of 'effects' that occur during the application of specific laboratory-based cognitive science experiments performed on higher education students to classrooms containing secondary age students. As a teacher, you should always be ready to challenge CPD that is presented to you, whether it is about learning styles or retrieval practice; if you perceive the session deliverer has not outlined the full level of limitations then it is your professional responsibility to call attention to this before it harms the learning of your students.

CURRICULUM AND ASSESSMENT CONSTRAINTS

Despite growing interest in learning sciences, curriculum and assessment structures often limit their full implementation. The emphasis on high-stakes testing and content coverage can discourage experimentation with creative pedagogical approaches that prioritise deep learning over surface memorisation. Additionally, while spaced learning is effective, rigid timetables and exam pressures may prevent teachers from revisiting topics in a spaced manner within an optimum timeframe. Furthermore, the integration of learning sciences into curriculum design remains limited. While some exam boards and curriculum frameworks acknowledge cognitive principles, they rarely provide explicit guidance on how to embed them systematically, which leaves teachers to navigate the tension between innovative practice and accountability measures. Teachers are expected to sort examination content into cued recall, near transfer and far transfer for themselves. This lack of support and focused CPD creates opportunities for students to be taught using the wrong kinds of methods leading to issues with their ability to pass examinations.

EQUITY AND ACCESS

Another challenge is ensuring that the benefits of learning sciences reach all students. Research-informed strategies can be powerful, but their effectiveness depends on contextual factors such as classroom environment, teacher expertise and student background. There is a risk that schools with more resources and access to research may implement these strategies more effectively, potentially widening existing inequalities.

For example, digital tools and AI engines that support retrieval practice or adaptive learning are more accessible in well-funded schools. Meanwhile, students in under-resourced settings may not benefit from the same level of innovation. This raises important questions about how learning sciences can be scaled equitably across diverse educational contexts.

CONCLUSION

In summary, the learning sciences have made significant inroads into secondary education, particularly through evidence-informed pedagogies and professional development. Teachers are increasingly aware of cognitive principles and their implications for classroom practice. However, systemic barriers, including curriculum constraints, uneven access to high-quality CPD and equity concerns, continue to limit their full potential. Reflecting on these challenges is essential as we consider how the field might evolve to better support teachers and learners in the future. What is clear is that the picture in schools is variable. Some schools use learning sciences accurately and purposefully, some use them incorrectly and some do not use them at all. It will be up to you to ensure your school is using these theories of learning in a way that delivers optimised learning for your students.

EMERGING TRENDS AND INNOVATIONS

As the learning sciences continue to evolve, they intersect with technological, pedagogical and interdisciplinary innovations that are reshaping secondary education. This section explores key emerging trends that are beginning to influence classroom practice, teacher roles and student experiences. While some of these developments are already underway, others remain speculative, but carry significant potential for transformation.

TECHNOLOGY-ENHANCED LEARNING

One of the most prominent trends is the integration of artificial intelligence (AI) and adaptive learning technologies into teaching and learning. Platforms such as Century Tech™ and Squirrel AI™ in the USA use machine-learning algorithms to personalise content delivery, identify misconceptions and provide real-time feedback. These systems draw on learning sciences principles, such as spaced repetition and formative assessment, to optimise learning pathways for individual students. For example, a teacher might use an AI-powered platform to assign tasks based on students' prior performance, allowing for targeted intervention and support. However, these technologies also raise questions about teacher agency, data privacy and the risk of over-reliance on algorithmic decision-making.

LEARNING ANALYTICS AND DATA-INFORMED PRACTICE

Closely related to AI is the rise of learning analytics, which involves collecting and analysing data on student behaviour, engagement and performance. These insights can help teachers make informed decisions about instruction, identify students who may need additional support and evaluate the effectiveness of pedagogical strategies. In some schools, dashboards provide visualisations of student progress, enabling teachers to spot patterns and intervene early. However, the use of data in education must be approached critically. As Williamson and Eynon (2020) argue, learning analytics can reinforce existing biases if not carefully designed and interpreted. Moreover, ethical concerns around student surveillance and consent must be addressed.

NEUROSCIENCE AND COGNITIVE ENHANCEMENT

The intersection of neuroscience and education continues to generate interest, though it remains a contested space. While some applications, such as understanding executive functions and working memory, have informed classroom strategies, in the past *neuromyths* such as learning styles or 'left-brain/right-brain' thinking have been perpetuated. Recent research has focused on how cognitive load theory and attention mechanisms can inform instructional design, for instance, reducing extraneous cognitive load in presentations or scaffolding complex tasks align with findings from cognitive neuroscience. However, translating neuroscience into practice requires caution and collaboration between researchers and teachers to avoid oversimplification, misapplication or implementation drift.

INTERDISCIPLINARY APPROACHES

The learning sciences are increasingly drawing on interdisciplinary frameworks, combining insights from psychology, computer science, design thinking and sociology. This shift encourages more holistic approaches to learning, where cognitive development is considered alongside social, emotional and cultural factors. For example, *design-based research* (DBR) methodologies allow teachers to co-create and test interventions in real-world settings, bridging the gap between theory and practice. DBR has been used to develop collaborative learning environments, enquiry-based science curricula and digital tools that support metacognition (Anderson and Shattuck, 2012).

STUDENT-CENTRED AND PARTICIPATORY LEARNING

Another emerging trend is the move towards student-centred learning, where learners have greater agency in shaping their educational experiences. This includes personalised learning pathways, project-based learning and co-construction of knowledge. Learning sciences support this shift by emphasising the importance of motivation, self-regulation and social interaction in learning. Some schools are now experimenting with flexible timetables and interest-driven modules, allowing students to pursue topics aligned with their passions while still meeting curriculum goals. These approaches require a rethinking of assessment, classroom management and teacher roles, but they align with research on intrinsic motivation and deep learning. While the number of schools that present learning like this are low in number, as the AI era fully evolves so more schools will begin to adopt this adaptive approach to learning.

The learning sciences are at the heart of several transformative trends in secondary education. From AI-driven personalisation to interdisciplinary research and student-centred pedagogies, these innovations offer exciting possibilities for enhancing learning. However, they also demand critical reflection, ethical scrutiny and thoughtful implementation. As we look to the future, it is essential that teachers remain engaged with emerging research, advocate for equitable access and retain professional autonomy in navigating these changes.

SPECULATING ON THE FUTURE

While the learning sciences have already begun to shape secondary education, their future influence may be even more profound. In this section, we explore speculative yet plausible scenarios that illustrate how learning sciences might evolve and transform teaching and learning in secondary schools. These scenarios are not predictions, but provocations, intended to stimulate reflection on the possibilities, challenges and ethical considerations that lie ahead.

SCENARIO 1: AI-AUGMENTED CLASSROOMS

Imagine a classroom where artificial intelligence (AI) systems work alongside teachers to deliver personalised learning experiences. AI tutors provide real-time feedback, adapt content to individual learning profiles and even monitor emotional engagement through biometric data. Teachers, in turn, shift from content delivery to roles as learning designers, mentors and data interpreters.

This scenario builds on current developments in adaptive learning platforms and learning analytics (Holmes et al., 2019). For example, platforms like AltSchool™ and IBM Watson Education™ have already piloted AI-driven personalisation, with AltSchool reporting a 25 per cent increase in student engagement and IBM Watson supporting predictive analytics to guide instruction. Similarly, tools like Quizlet™ use adaptive algorithms to prioritise areas needing improvement, resulting in a 40 per cent boost in retention. This scenario aligns with learning sciences principles such as formative assessment, cognitive load management and metacognitive scaffolding. However, it also raises critical questions:

- how do we ensure teacher autonomy in AI-mediated environments?

- what safeguards are needed to protect student data privacy and emotional well-being?

- will AI systems reinforce existing biases or challenge them?

The future of AI in education will depend not only on technological capability, but also on ethical governance, inclusive design and professional development that empowers teachers to use these tools critically.

SCENARIO 2: REIMAGINED ASSESSMENT

Assessment is often cited as a barrier to innovation in education. But what if learning sciences helped us reimagine it entirely? In this scenario, traditional exams are replaced by continuous, multimodal assessment that captures learning over time through portfolios, peer feedback and performance tasks. Natural language processing tools assess reasoning and creativity, while analytics track growth in metacognitive and collaborative skills.

This vision draws on research into formative assessment, self-regulated learning and authentic assessment (Black and Wiliam, 2009; Nicol and Macfarlane-Dick, 2006). It also reflects practices already underway in initiatives like Harvard Project Zero™, where teachers design assessments around concepts such as 'greatness' or 'perspective', using student reflections, video documentation and peer critique to capture learning as it unfolds.

These practices align with learning sciences principles by embedding assessment within the learning process and positioning students as co-constructors of meaning. This scenario reflects a growing recognition that standardised testing often fails to capture the complexity of learning. However, implementing such a system would require:

- a shift in policy and accountability frameworks;

- investment in teacher training and assessment literacy;

- robust mechanisms to ensure fairness, transparency and accessibility.

Learning sciences can provide the theoretical foundation for this transformation, but systemic change will be essential to make it viable.

SCENARIO 3: RADICAL PERSONALISATION AND LEARNER AGENCY

In a third scenario, students navigate personalised learning pathways tailored to their cognitive profiles, interests and goals. Drawing on insights from neuroscience, psychology and data science, these pathways adapt dynamically to support optimal challenge and engagement. Students co-design their learning experiences, choosing from modular curricula and interdisciplinary projects. This approach reflects the learning sciences' emphasis on motivation, agency and contextualised learning (Ryan and Deci, 2000; Sawyer, 2014). Real-world models such as *competency-based education* (CBE) and *project-based learning* (PBL) already embody aspects of this vision. CBE allows students to progress by demonstrating mastery rather than seat time, improving graduation rates by 20 per cent. PBL connects learning to students' interests and real-world problems, boosting retention by up to 85 per cent. Some schools also experiment with flexible timetables and digital portfolios, enabling students to manage their learning schedules and reflect on progress. This scenario resonates with constructivist and sociocultural theories that view learning as a participatory, meaning-making process, yet radical personalisation poses risks. It:

- could lead to fragmentation of knowledge and loss of shared educational experiences;

- might exacerbate inequities if some students receive richer learning opportunities than others;

- raises the matter of how we balance individual agency with collective responsibility and citizenship education.

These issues highlight the need for thoughtful design and inclusive policy frameworks that ensure personalisation enhances, not undermines, educational equity and coherence.

IMPLICATIONS FOR TEACHERS AND SCHOOLS

Across these scenarios, the role of the teacher is transformed. Teachers become facilitators of enquiry, curators of resources and interpreters of data. Their professional identity shifts from content expert to learning architect, requiring new forms of expertise and collaboration.

Schools, too, may evolve into learning hubs that blend formal and informal education, integrate community partnerships and support lifelong learning. The boundaries between subjects, year groups and even physical classrooms may become more fluid. To prepare for these futures, teachers will need:

- access to ongoing professional learning grounded in the learning sciences;

- opportunities to co-create innovations with researchers, technologists and students;

- supportive leadership and policy environments that value experimentation, reflection and ethical practice.

Speculating on the future of learning sciences in secondary education invites us to imagine bold possibilities and confront complex dilemmas. Whether through AI augmentation, reimagined assessment, or radical personalisation, the learning sciences offer tools and frameworks to guide innovation. But their impact will depend on how we navigate questions of equity, ethics and professional agency. As teachers, researchers and policy-makers, we must shape these futures deliberately, ensuring that learning remains a human, relational and transformative endeavour.

CRITICAL REFLECTIONS AND ETHICAL CONSIDERATIONS

As the learning sciences increasingly influence secondary education, it is essential to reflect critically on the ethical dimensions of their application. While these innovations offer powerful tools for enhancing learning, they also introduce complex dilemmas around data privacy, equity and teacher autonomy. This section explores some of the most pressing ethical considerations that must be addressed as we move forward.

DATA PRIVACY AND SURVEILLANCE

The rise of AI, learning analytics and biometric technologies in education raises significant concerns about student data privacy. Systems that track engagement, emotional states, or cognitive performance often collect sensitive information, sometimes without explicit consent or clear understanding from students and families. As Sälzer and Prenzel (2019) argue, the use of big data in education must be governed by transparent policies that prioritise student rights, informed consent and data minimisation. Moreover, the potential for surveillance, whether through classroom cameras, keystroke monitoring, or predictive analytics, poses risks to student well-being and autonomy. Ethical implementation requires robust safeguards, clear accountability structures and ongoing dialogue with stakeholders.

EQUITY AND INCLUSION

Learning sciences have the potential to reduce educational disparities, but only if their benefits are distributed equitably. Access to research-informed tools and technologies often depends on school funding, infrastructure and teacher expertise. Without deliberate efforts to address these gaps, innovations may inadvertently widen the digital divide, privileging students in well-resourced schools while leaving others behind; for example, adaptive learning platforms may personalise instruction effectively, but only if students have reliable access to devices and connectivity. Similarly, professional development in learning sciences must be inclusive, ensuring that all teachers, not just those in elite networks, can engage with and apply emerging research.

TEACHER AGENCY AND PROFESSIONAL ETHICS

As technologies become more embedded in classrooms, there is a risk that teacher agency may be diminished. Automated systems that recommend instructional strategies or assess student work can undermine professional judgement if used uncritically. Teachers must remain central to decision-making, interpreting data through the lens of pedagogical expertise and contextual knowledge.

Ethical practice also involves resisting reductive applications of learning sciences, such as using cognitive science to justify rigid behaviourist models or ignoring the social and emotional dimensions of learning. A balanced approach recognises the complexity of teaching and values the relational, human aspects of education.

Ethical considerations are not peripheral to the future of learning sciences – they are foundational. As we embrace innovation, we must also cultivate critical literacy, inclusive design and ethical reflexivity. By foregrounding these principles, teachers can ensure that learning sciences serve not only to enhance outcomes, but also to uphold values of fairness, dignity and professional integrity.

CONSIDER THIS: ACADEMIC ACCURACY AND AUTHENTICITY

Considering the idea that most schools now openly declare they are using learning sciences, reflect on the ideas pertaining to academic accuracy and authenticity presented in this chapter. In reflecting on this, think about the following.

- How do schools and trusts ensure that the ideas and evidence which they draw upon when drafting processes and policies are both accurate and reflect the latest developments?

- What barriers do schools and trusts have to ensuring that the quality of academic work they use or have access to is of the quality used by universities across the world?

- How can schools or trusts reflect on and review established policies and processes that were developed and introduced in the earlier stages of when schools began to use learning sciences, where errors, misconceptions or outdated evidence might be present?

- How can schools and trusts ensure that they create sufficient capacity for autonomy within teaching staff so that policies and processes drawn from learning sciences ideas undergo a degree of criticality at the level of implementation?

CHAPTER SUMMARY

This chapter has explored the evolving role of the learning sciences in secondary school teaching, tracing their current influence, emerging innovations and speculative futures. From the integration of cognitive science into everyday pedagogy to the rise of AI-driven personalisation and interdisciplinary approaches, the learning sciences offer a rich foundation for reimagining education.

Reflecting on current practice reveals both progress and persistent challenges. Evidence-informed strategies such as retrieval practice and metacognition are increasingly embedded in classrooms, yet systemic constraints, such as curriculum rigidity, inequitable access and limited professional development, continue to hinder their full potential. Emerging trends, including adaptive technologies, learning analytics and student-centred design promise to deepen and diversify learning experiences, but they also demand critical scrutiny.

Speculating on the future invites us to consider bold possibilities: AI-augmented classrooms, reimagined assessment systems and radically personalised learning pathways. These scenarios highlight the transformative potential of the learning sciences, while also surfacing ethical tensions around data privacy, equity and teacher agency. As teachers, we must engage with these futures not passively, but proactively, shaping them through reflective practice, collaborative enquiry and principled decision-making.

Ultimately, the future of learning sciences in secondary education is not predetermined. It will be shaped by the choices we make today: how we interpret research, how we design learning environments and how we advocate for inclusive, ethical and empowering educational practices. By remaining critically engaged and professionally curious, teachers can ensure that the learning sciences serve not only to improve outcomes, but also to enrich the human experience of learning itself.

REFLECTIVE QUESTIONS: CHAPTER 12

The questions below encourage you to think about the translation of theory into practice and how to balance evidence-informed strategies with contextual sensitivity, especially in classrooms with varied learning profiles and backgrounds.

- How can you critically evaluate and apply learning sciences research in your own classroom practice, while remaining responsive to the diverse needs of your students?

- What ethical responsibilities do you have when using educational technologies and data-driven tools to support learning, and how can you ensure these tools are used equitably and transparently?

- In what ways might your role as a teacher evolve in response to emerging trends in the learning sciences; how can you prepare to navigate these changes with confidence and integrity?

FURTHER READING

ITTECF 8.7 Engaging in high quality professional development can help teachers improve.

Cordingley, P., Higgins, S., Greany, T., Buckler, N., Coles-Jordan, D., Crisp, B., Saunders, L. and Coe, R. (2015) *Developing Great Teaching*. Available at: https://tdtrust.org/about/dgt. Accessed 24 November 2025.

This report was commissioned against a backdrop of concerns regarding the variable quality of professional development (CPD) opportunities in England. Feedback indicated that CPD was often narrowly viewed, not focused on pupil needs, lacked sustainment and was not practice-based. This aligns with OECD TALIS 2013 findings that English teachers participate more in short courses but less in in-depth activities. The government aimed to support quality, evidence-based CPD, leading to this review.

REFERENCES

Anderson, T. and Shattuck, J. (2012). Design-based research: a decade of progress in education research? *Educational Researcher, 41*(1), 16–25. https://doi.org/10.3102/0013189X11428813

Black, P. and Wiliam, D. (2009). Developing the theory of formative assessment. *Educational Assessment, Evaluation and Accountability, 21*(1), 5–31. https://doi.org/10.1007/s11092-008-9068-5

Bransford, J. D., Brown, A. L. and Cocking, R. R. (eds) (2000). *How People Learn: Brain, Mind, Experience, and School*. Washington, DC: National Academy Press.

Deans for Impact (2015). *The Science of Learning.* Available at: www.deansforimpact.org/files/assets/thescienceoflearning.pdf. Accessed 24 November 2025.

Dunlosky, J., Rawson, K. A., Marsh, E. J., Nathan, M. J. and Willingham, D. T. (2013). Improving students' learning with effective learning techniques: promising directions from cognitive and educational psychology. *Psychological Science in the Public Interest, 14*(1), 4–58. https://doi.org/10.1177/1529100612453266

Education Endowment Foundation (EEF) (2018). *Metacognition and Self-Regulated Learning: Guidance Report.* Available at: https://educationendowmentfoundation.org.uk/education-evidence/guidance-reports/metacognition. Accessed 24 November 2025.

EEF (2021). *Teaching and Learning Toolkit.* Available at: https://educationendowmentfoundation.org.uk/education-evidence/teaching-learning-toolkit. Accessed 24 November 2025.

Holmes, W., Bialik, M. and Fadel, C. (2019). *Artificial Intelligence in Education: Promises and Implications for Teaching and Learning.* Boston, MA: Center for Curriculum Redesign.

Nicol, D. and Macfarlane-Dick, D. (2006). Formative assessment and self-regulated learning: a model and seven principles of good feedback practice. *Studies in Higher Education, 31*(2), 199–218. https://doi.org/10.1080/03075070600572090

Ryan, R. M. and Deci, E. L. (2000). Self-determination theory and the facilitation of intrinsic motivation, social development, and well-being. *American Psychologist, 55*(1), 68–78. https://doi.org/10.1037/0003-066X.55.1.68

Sälzer, C. and Prenzel, M. (2019). Big data and education: ethical challenges. In R. Gorur, S. Sellar and G. Steiner-Khamsi (eds), *Big Data in Education.* Heidelberg: Springer, pp. 145–60.

Sawyer, R. K. (ed.) (2014). *The Cambridge Handbook of the Learning Sciences*, 2nd edn. Cambridge: Cambridge University Press. https://doi.org/10.1017/CBO9781139519526

Williamson, B. and Eynon, R. (2020). Historical threads, missing links, and future directions in AI in education. *Learning, Media and Technology, 45*(3), 223–35. https://doi.org/10.1080/17439884.2020.1798995

INDEX